Jan Peters

Machine Learning for Robotics

D1160764

Jan Peters

Machine Learning for Robotics

Learning Methods for Robot Motor Skills

VDM Verlag Dr. Müller

Imprint

Bibliographic information by the German National Library: The German National Library lists this publication at the German National Bibliography; detailed bibliographic information is available on the Internet at http://dnb.d-nb.de.

Any brand names and product names mentioned in this book are subject to trademark, brand or patent protection and are trademarks or registered trademarks of their respective holders. The use of brand names, product names, common names, trade names, product descriptions etc. even without a particular marking in this works is in no way to be construed to mean that such names may be regarded as unrestricted in respect of trademark and brand protection legislation and could thus be used by anyone.

Cover image: www.purestockx.com

Publisher:
VDM Verlag Dr. Müller Aktiengesellschaft & Co. KG, Dudweiler Landstr. 125 a, 66123 Saarbrücken, Germany,
Phone +49 681 9100-698, Fax +49 681 9100-988,
Email: info@vdm-verlag.de

Copyright © 2008 VDM Verlag Dr. Müller Aktiengesellschaft & Co. KG and licensors
All rights reserved. Saarbrücken 2008

Produced in USA and UK by:
Lightning Source Inc., La Vergne, Tennessee, USA
Lightning Source UK Ltd., Milton Keynes, UK
BookSurge LLC, 5341 Dorchester Road, Suite 16, North Charleston, SC 29418, USA

ISBN: 978-3-639-02110-3

Acknowledgments

This book would have never been possible without initiation, continuing encouragement, coordination, supervision and understanding help of *Stefan Schaal.* He is a great 'sensei' and has endured my research roller-coaster ride from my masters book to today. Another thanks goes to *Firdaus Udwadia* and *Sethu Vijayakumar* from whom both I learned a lot on analytical dynamics and machine learning, respectively. I am also very grateful to the committee members, i.e., *Stefan Schaal, Gaurav Sukhatme, Firdaus Udwadia* and *Chris Atkeson* for reading my book and participating in the defense. I am indebted to *Mitsuo Kawato* and *Gordon Cheng* who made two stays in 2000 and 2003 at the Advanced Telecommunication Research Center ATR in Kyoto, Japan, possible. Without the first visit in 2000, I would have never met Stefan Schaal and my life would have taken a very different turn. Finally, I have to thank all my friends and family for leading me to a career in science and continuing support. My girl-friend *Ayşenur Altingül* for her understanding and love. Another thanks goes to my friends from USC learning labs i.e., *Aaron d'Souza, Aude Billard, Auke Ijspeert, Dimitris Pongas, Jun Nakanishi, Michael Mistry, Nerses Ohanyan, Peyman Mohajerian, Rick Cory, Sethu Viyahakumar, Srideep Musuvathy, Vidhya Navalpakkam* and many more, for all the advice, support, help, and ... the good times and great parties!

Table of Contents

List Of Tables

List Of Figures

Abbreviations

In this book we use the following mathematical notation throughout this book:

Notation	**Description**
$\{x_1, x_2, \ldots, x_n\}$	set with elements $x_1, x_2, \ldots, x_n$
$\mathbb{R}$	real numbers
$\mathbf{x} = [x_1, x_2, \ldots, x_n]$	a vector
x_i	the i-th component of the vector $\mathbf{x}$
$\mathbf{A} = [\mathbf{a}_1, \mathbf{a}_2, \ldots, \mathbf{a}_m]$	a matrix
$\mathbf{a}_i$	the i-th vector of a matrix $\mathbf{A}$
a_{ij}	the i, j-th component of the matrix $\mathbf{A}$
$\mathbf{A}^{-1}$	matrix inverse
$\mathbf{A}^{+}$	matrix pseudo-inverse
$\mathbf{A}^{1/2}$	matrix root
$\boldsymbol{\nabla}_{\theta_i} f$	derivative with respect to parameter θ_i
$\boldsymbol{\nabla}_{\boldsymbol{\theta}} f$	derivative with respect to parameters θ_i
$\frac{\partial f}{\partial q}$	partial derivative
$p(\mathbf{x})$	probability density of $\mathbf{x}$
$E\{\mathbf{x}\}$	expectation of $\mathbf{x}$
$\bar{\mathbf{x}} = \langle \mathbf{x} \rangle$	sample average of $\mathbf{x}$

As symbols in this book, the following symbols will be used in several chapters.

Symbol	**Description**
$\pi(\mathbf{u}\|\mathbf{x})$	control policy
$r(\mathbf{x}, \mathbf{u})$	reward
$U(r)$	utility transformation of a reward
$J(\boldsymbol{\theta})$	expected return
$Q^{\pi}(\mathbf{x}, \mathbf{u}), V^{\pi}(\mathbf{x})$	value functions of policy π
$d^{\pi}(\mathbf{x})$	state distribution under policy π
$\mathbf{F}_{\boldsymbol{\theta}}$	Fisher information matrix
$d_{\mathrm{KL}}(\theta', \theta) = d_{\mathrm{KL}}(p_{\theta'}(\boldsymbol{\tau}) \|\| p_{\theta}(\boldsymbol{\tau}))$	Kullback-Leibler divergence
$\boldsymbol{\nabla}_{\boldsymbol{\theta}} J$	'vanilla' policy gradient
$\widetilde{\boldsymbol{\nabla}}_{\boldsymbol{\theta}} J$	natural policy gradient

Symbol	Description
t	time (continuous)
$\mathbf{x}$	task space position, state of the task
$\dot{\mathbf{x}}, \ddot{\mathbf{x}}$	task space velocity, acceleration
$\ddot{\mathbf{x}}_{\text{ref}}$	reference acceleration
$\mathbf{q}, \dot{\mathbf{q}}, \ddot{\mathbf{q}}$	joint position, velocity,acceleration
$\mathbf{q}_d, \dot{\mathbf{q}}_d, \ddot{\mathbf{q}}_d$	desired joint position, velocity,acceleration
$\mathbf{u}$	motor command, action
$\mathbf{x}_{1:H}$	series of states $\mathbf{x}_i$ with $i \in \{1, 2, \dots, H\}$
$\mathbf{u}_{1:H}$	series of actions $\mathbf{u}_i$ with $i \in \{1, 2, \dots, H\}$
$\boldsymbol{\tau} = [\mathbf{x}_{1:H}, \mathbf{u}_{1:H}]$	rollout, trajectory, sampe path, history
$\mathbf{M}(\mathbf{q})$	inertia matrices
$\mathbf{F}(\mathbf{q}, \dot{\mathbf{q}}), \mathbf{F}(\mathbf{q}, \dot{\mathbf{q}}, t)$	internal forces
$\mathbf{G}(\mathbf{q})$	gravity
$\mathbf{C}(\mathbf{q}, \dot{\mathbf{q}})$	Coriolis and centripetal forces
$\varepsilon(\mathbf{q}, \dot{\mathbf{q}})$	unmodeled nonlinearities
$h(\mathbf{q}, \dot{\mathbf{q}}, t) = 0$	constraint task description
$\mathbf{A}(\mathbf{x}, \dot{\mathbf{x}})\ddot{\mathbf{x}} = b(\mathbf{x}, \dot{\mathbf{x}})$, $\mathbf{A}\ddot{\mathbf{x}} = b$	differential constraint task description
$\mathbf{N}$	arbitrary metric
$K_P = [\kappa_{ij}], K_D = [\delta_{ij}]$	gains of a PD control law

Abstract

Autonomous robots that can assist humans in situations of daily life have been a long standing vision of robotics, artificial intelligence, and cognitive sciences. A first step towards this goal is to create robots that can accomplish a multitude of different tasks, triggered by environmental context or higher level instruction. Early approaches to this goal during the heydays of artificial intelligence research in the late 1980s, however, made it clear that an approach purely based on reasoning and human insights would not be able to model all the perceptuomotor tasks that a robot should fulfill. Instead, new hope was put in the growing wake of machine learning that promised fully adaptive control algorithms which learn both by observation and trial-and-error. However, to date, learning techniques have yet to fulfill this promise as only few methods manage to scale into the high-dimensional domains of manipulator robotics, or even the new upcoming trend of humanoid robotics, and usually scaling was only achieved in precisely pre-structured domains. In this book, we investigate the ingredients for a general approach to motor skill learning in order to get one step closer towards human-like performance. For doing so, we study two major components for such an approach, i.e., firstly, a theoretically well-founded general approach to representing the required control structures for task representation and execution and, secondly, appropriate learning algorithms which can be applied in this setting.

As a theoretical foundation, we first study a general framework to generate control laws for real robots with a particular focus on skills represented as dynamical systems in differential constraint form. We present a point-wise optimal control framework resulting from a generalization of Gauss' principle and show how various well-known robot control laws can be derived by modifying the metric of the employed cost function. The framework has been successfully applied to task space tracking control for holonomic systems for several different metrics on the anthropomorphic SARCOS Master Arm.

In order to overcome the limiting requirement of accurate robot models, we first employ learning methods to find learning controllers for task space control. However, when learning to execute a redundant control problem, we face the general problem of the non-convexity of the solution space which can force the robot to steer into physically impossible configurations if supervised learning methods are employed without further consideration. This problem can be resolved using two major insights, i.e., the learning problem can be treated as locally convex and the cost function of the analytical framework can be used to ensure global consistency. Thus, we derive an immediate reinforcement learning algorithm from the expectation-maximization point of view which leads to a reward-weighted regression technique. This method can be used both for operational space control as well as general immediate reward reinforcement learning problems. We demonstrate the feasibility of the resulting framework on the problem of redundant end-effector tracking for both a simulated 3 degrees of freedom robot arm as well as for a simulated anthropomorphic SARCOS Master Arm.

While learning to execute tasks in task space is an essential component to a general framework to motor skill learning, learning the actual task is of even higher importance, particularly as this issue is more frequently beyond the abilities of analytical approaches than execution. We focus on the learning of elemental tasks which can serve as the "building blocks of movement generation", called motor primitives. Motor primitives are parameterized task representations based on splines or nonlinear differential equations with desired attractor properties. While imitation learning of parameterized motor primitives is a relatively well-understood problem, the self-improvement by interaction of the system with the environment remains a challenging problem, tackled in the fourth chapter of this book. For pursuing this goal, we highlight the difficulties with current reinforcement learning methods, and outline both established and novel algorithms for the gradient-based improvement of parameterized policies. We compare these algorithms in the context of motor primitive learning, and show that our most modern algorithm, the Episodic Natural Actor-Critic outperforms previous algorithms by at least an order of magnitude. We demonstrate the efficiency of this reinforcement learning method in the application of learning to hit a baseball with an anthropomorphic robot arm.

In conclusion, in this book, we have contributed a general framework for analytically computing robot control laws which can be used for deriving various previous control approaches and serves as foundation as well as inspiration for our learning algorithms. We have introduced two classes of novel reinforcement learning methods, i.e., the Natural Actor-Critic and the Reward-Weighted Regression algorithm. These algorithms have been used in order to replace the analytical components of the theoretical framework by learned representations. Evaluations have been performed on both simulated and real robot arms.

Chapter 1

Introduction

Knowledge and scientific insight are the joy
and the entitlement for the existence of all humanity.
Alexander von Humboldt (Prussian naturalist, 1769-1859)

1.1 Motivation

Despite an increasing number of motor skills exhibited by manipulator and humanoid robots, the general approach to the generation of such motor behaviors has changed little over the last decades (Tsai, 1999; Craig, 2005; Sciavicco & Siciliano, 2007; De Wit, Siciliano, & Bastin, 1996). The roboticist models the task as accurately as possible and uses human understanding of the required motor skills in order to create the desired robot behavior as well as to eliminate all uncertainties of the environment. In most cases, such a process boils down to recording a desired trajectory in a pre-structured environment with precisely placed objects. If inaccuracies remain, the engineer creates exceptions using human understanding of the task. In order to be controllable, the robot tracking the trajectory is usually a heavy structure with non-backdrivable, noncompliant joints resulting in high-payload to weight ratio, low energy-efficiency and dangers for its environment (Hirzinger et al., 2002; Sciavicco & Siciliano, 2007). While such highly engineered approaches are feasible in well-structured industrial or research environments, it is obvious that if robots should ever leave factory floors and research environments, we will need to reduce or eliminate the complete reliance on hand-crafted models of the environment and the robots exhibited to date. Instead, we need a general approach which allows us to use compliant robots designed for interaction with less structured and uncertain environments in order to reach domains outside industry. Such an approach cannot solely rely on human understanding of the task but instead has to be acquired and adapted from data generated both by human demonstrations of the skill as well as trial and error of the robot.

The tremendous progress in machine learning over the last decades offers us the promise of less human-driven approaches to motor skill acquisition. However, despite offering the most general way of thinking about data-driven acquisition of motor skills, generic machine learning techniques, which do not rely on an understanding of motor systems, often do not scale into the domain of manipulator or humanoid robotics due to the high domain dimensionality. Therefore, instead of attempting an unstructured, monolithic machine learning approach to motor skill aquisition, we need to develop approaches suitable for this particular domain with the inherent problems of task representation, learning and execution addressed separately in a coherent framework. Such a general architecture needs to be developed from the perspective of analytical motor control and employing a combination of imitation, reinforcement and model learning in order to cope with the complexities involved in motor skill learning. The advantage of such a concerted approach is that it allows the separation of the main problems of motor skill acquisition, refinement and control. Instead of either having an unstructured, monolithic machine learning approach or creating hand-crafted approaches with pre-specified trajectories, we are capable of aquiring skills from demonstrations and refine them using trial and error. The creation and improvement of such skills takes place through a combination of imitation and reinforcement learning. The acquired skills are represented as policies and can principally include specifications ranging from positions, velocities and acceleration to applied forces, stiffnesses, etc. When using learning-based approaches for control instead of analytical models of the robots dynamics and kinematics, we often can achieve accurate control without needing to model the complete system by hand. Furthermore, robots no longer need to be built with the focus on being straightforward to model but can be chosen to fulfill the tasks requirements in terms of compliance with the environment, energy efficiency, and other factors.

1.2 Objective and Approach

The principal objective of this book is to move closer towards a general learning architecture for motor skills, i.e., to tackle the question

> **"How can we find a general framework for representing, learning and executing motor skills for robotics?"**

As can be observed from this question, the major goal of this book requires three building blocks, i.e., (i) appropriate representations for movements, (ii) learning algorithms which can be applied to these representations and (iii) a transformation which allows the execution of the kinematic plans in the respective task space on robots. These essential components will be discussed in detail in Section 1.2.1 while the resulting idea for a general approach is discussed in Section 1.2.2.

1.2.1 Essential Components

In order to make a step towards the objective of finding a general framework for motor skills, we have to address our basic philosophy towards the three essential components, i.e., representation, learning and execution. In this section, we briefly outline on which fundamental concepts we will be building on in this book and how the different topics relate to each other.

Representation. For the representation of motor skills, we can rely on the insight that humans, while being capable of performing a large variety of complicated movements, restrict themselves to a smaller amount of primitive motions (Schaal, Ijspeert, & Billard, 2004). As suggested by Ijspeert et al. (2002, 2003), such primitive movements can be represented by nonlinear dynamic systems. We can represent these in the differential constraint form given by

$$\mathbf{A}_{\boldsymbol{\theta}_i}(\mathbf{x}_i, \dot{\mathbf{x}}_i, t)\ddot{\mathbf{x}} = \mathbf{b}_{\boldsymbol{\theta}_i}(\mathbf{x}_i, \dot{\mathbf{x}}_i, t), \tag{1.1}$$

where $i \in \mathbb{N}$ is the index of the motor primitive in a library of movements, $\boldsymbol{\theta}_i \in \mathbb{R}^L$ denote the parameters of the primitive i, t denotes time and $\mathbf{x}_i$,$\dot{\mathbf{x}}_i$,$\ddot{\mathbf{x}}_i \in \mathbb{R}^n$ denote positions, velocities and accelerations of the dynamic system, respectively.

Learning. Learning basic motor skills[1] is achieved by adapting the parameters $\boldsymbol{\theta}_i$ of motor primitive i. The high dimensionality of our domain prohibits the exploration of the complete space of all admissible motor behaviors, rendering the application of machine learning techniques which require exhaustive exploration impossible. Instead, we have to rely on a combination of supervised and reinforcement learning in order to aquire motor skills where the supervised learning is used in order to obtain the initialization of the motor skill while reinforcement learning is used in order to improve it. Therefore, the aquisition of a novel motor task consists out of two phases,i.e., the 'learning robot' attempts to reproduce the skill acquired through supervised learning and improve the skill from experience by trial-and-error, i.e., through reinforcement learning.

Execution. The execution of motor skills adds another level of complexity. It requires that a mechanical system

$$\mathbf{u} = \mathbf{M}(\mathbf{q}, \dot{\mathbf{q}}, t)\ddot{\mathbf{q}} + \mathbf{F}(\mathbf{q}, \dot{\mathbf{q}}, t), \tag{1.2}$$

with a mapping $\mathbf{x}_i = \mathbf{f}_i(\mathbf{q}, \dot{\mathbf{q}}, t)$ can be forced to execute each motor primitive $\mathbf{A}_i\ddot{\mathbf{x}}_i = \mathbf{b}_i$ in order to fulfill the skill. The motor primitive can be viewed as a mechanical constraint acting upon the system, enforced through accurate computation of the required forces based on analytical models. However, in most cases it is very difficult to obtain accurate

[1] Learning by sequencing and parallelization of the motor primitives will be treated in future work.

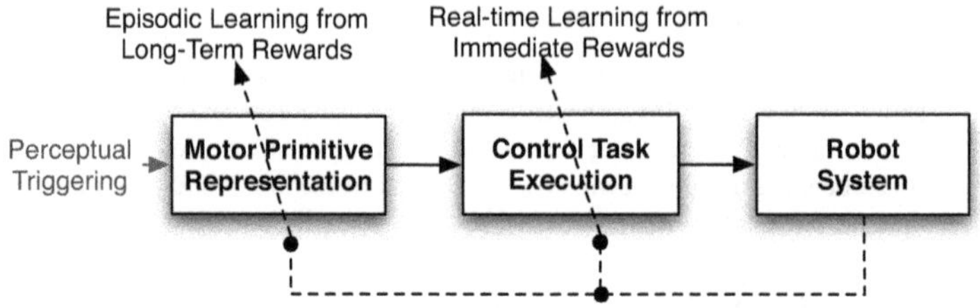

Figure 1.1: This figure illustrates our general approach to motor skill learning by dividing it into motor primitive and a motor control component. For the task execution, fast policy learning methods based on observable error need to be employed while the task learning is based on slower episodic learning.

models of the mechanical system. Therefore it can be more suitable to find a policy learning approach which replaces the control law based on the hand-crafted rigid body model. In this book, we will follow this approach which forms the basis for understanding motor skill learning.

1.2.2 Resulting Approach

As we have outlined during the discussion of our objective and its essential components, we require an appropriate general motor skill framework which allows us to separate the desired task-space movement generation (represented by the motor primitives) from movement control in the respective actuator space. We need to be able to understand this transformation from an analytical point of view and need to be able to relate it to general techniques in robotics. The resulting framework has to yield the execution component discussed before as well as a basic understanding for resulting learning frameworks. When turning the analytical approach into a learning framework, we have to consider two components, i.e., we need to determine how to learn the desired behavior represented by the motor primitives as well as the execution represented by the transformation of the motor primitives into motor commands. We need to develop scalable learning algorithms which are both appropriate and efficient when used with the chosen general motor skill learning architecture. Furthermore, we require algorithms for fast immediate policy learning for movement control based on instantly observable rewards in order to enable the system to cope with real-time improvement during the execution. The learning of the task itself on the other hand requires the learning of policies which define the long-term evolution of the task, i.e., motor primitives, which are learned on a trial-by-trial basis with episodic improvement using a teacher for demonstration and reinforcement learning for self-improvement. The resulting general concept underlying this book is illustrated in Figure 1.1.

1.3 Major Contributions

In this book, we have made progress towards a general framework for representing, learning and executing motor skills while demonstrating the application of this work to physical and simulated robots. This progress includes contributions to three different but related lines of research, i.e.,

- Machine Learning,
- Motor Skill Representation and Control,
- Robot Application,

hence the name of this book is "*Machine Learning for Motor Skills in Robotics*".

The problem of motor skills learning for robotics is obviously not solved before we have humanoid robots are to successfully perform most common motor tasks in people's homes. Nevertheless, we have made significant progress and several major contributions which we will outline in the next paragraphs. Each of these novel results can be seen as contribution to all three disciplines and together they can be seen as in a coherent and general basis for learning motor skills for robotics.

1.3.1 General, Unifying Framework

As mentioned before, our push for new motor skills largely relies upon a general unifying framework for a class of point-wise optimal control approaches. This framework allows us to derive previous and novel control approaches, e.g., for operational space control, and it serves as the basis for our learning framework.

Point-Wise Optimal Control Approach. For obtaining our generic framework, we start with the general insight by Udwadia (1996, 2003) that Nature enforces constraints on mechanical or structural systems in the similar way to a nonlinear controller and thus we can obtain control laws in a similar fashion. We formalize this basic insight for robotics with a particular focus on redundant degrees-of-freedom (DOFs) systems and rely on general understanding of the control framework as a special class of point-wise optimal controllers derived from differential constraints. We discuss resulting requirements for stability as well as an extension for hierarchical task prioritization. In a more limited case, it can be justified from the viewpoint from an infinite horizon point of view.

Unification of previous approaches. The suggested approach offers a promising unification and simplification of nonlinear control law design for robots obeying rigid body dynamics equations, both with or without external constraints. We take this line of reasoning one step further and demonstrate that several well-known and also novel nonlinear robot control laws can be derived from this generic methodology. We show experimental verifications on a Sarcos Master Arm robot for some of the the derived controllers.

1.3.2 Novel Learning Algorithms

As outlined before, we need two different styles of policy learning algorithms, i.e., methods for long-term reward optimization and methods for immediate improvement. Thus, we have developed two different classes of algorithms, i.e., the Natural Actor-Critic and the Reward-Weighted Regression.

Natural Actor-Critic. The Natural Actor-Critic algorithms (Peters, Vijayakumar, & Schaal, 2003a, 2005) are the fastest policy gradient methods to date and "the current method of choice" (Aberdeen, 2006). They rely on the insight that we need to maximize the reward while keeping the loss of experience constant, i.e., we need to measure the distance between our current path distribution and the new path distribution created by the policy. This distance can be measured by the Kullback-Leibler divergence and approximated using the Fisher information metric resulting in a natural policy gradient approach. This natural policy gradient has a connection to the recently introduced compatible function approximation, which allows to obtain the Natural Actor-Critic. Interestingly, earlier Actor-Critic approaches can be derived from this new approach. In application to motor primitive learning, we can demonstrate that the Natural Actor-Critic outperforms both finite-difference gradients as well as 'vanilla' policy gradient methods with optimal baselines.

Reward-Weighted Regression. In contrast to the gradient-based Natural Actor-Critic algorithms, the Reward-Weighted Regression algorithm (Peters & Schaal, 2006a, 2007a, 2007b) focuses on immediate reward improvement and employs an adaptation of the expectation maximization (EM) algorithm for reinforcement learning. The key difference here is that when using immediate rewards, we can learn from our actions directly, i.e., use them as training examples similar to a supervised learning problem with a higher priority for samples with a higher reward. Thus, this problem is a reward-weighted regression problem, i.e., it has a well-defined solution which can be obtained using established regression techniques. While we have given a more intuitive explanation of this algorithm, it corresponds to a properly derived maximization-maximization (MM) algorithm which maximizes a lower bound on the immediate reward similar to an EM algorithm. It can be shown to scale to high dimensional domains and learn a good policy without any imitation of a human teacher.

1.3.3 Robot Application

The general setup presented in this book can be applied in robotics using analytical models as well as the presented learning algorithms. The applications presented in this book include motor primitive learning and operational space control.

Operational Space Control. Operational space control is one of the more general frameworks for obtaining task-level control laws in robotics. In this book, we present two new contributions to this field. First, we show how both well-established as well as novel task-space tracking algorithms can be obtained by posing the problem as a task-space constraint and simply varying the metric in the point-wise cost function given by our general framework. We can show that all of the presented methods result in roughly the same quality of tracking performance but that the resulting joint-space trajectories differ significantly due to the shifted force distribution on the joints.

Our second contribution is a learning framework for operational space control which is a result of both the general point-wise optimal control framework and our insight into immediate reward reinforcement learning. While the general learning of operational space controllers with redundant degrees of freedom is non-convex and thus global supervised learning techniques cannot be applied straightforwardly, we can gain two insights, i.e., that the problem is locally convex and that our point-wise cost function allows us to ensure global consistency among the local solutions. We show that this can yield the analytically determined optimal solution for simulated three degrees of freedom arms where we can sample the state-space sufficiently. Similarly, we can show the framework works for simulations of the anthropomorphic SARCOS Master Arm.

Motor Primitive Improvement. The main application of our long-term improvement framework is the optimization of motor primitives. Here, we follow essentially the previously outlined idea of acquiring an initial solution by supervised learning and then using reinforcement learning for motor primitive improvement. For this, we demonstrate both comparisons of motor primitive learning with different policy gradient methods, i.e., finite difference methods, 'vanilla' policy gradient methods and the Natural Actor-Critic, as well as an application of the most successful method, the Natural Actor-Critic to T-Ball learning.

1.4 Book Outline

In the last section of this introduction, we will briefly outline the structure and connections between the remaining chapters. The relation between the book structure and the different chapters of this book proposal is given in Figure 1.4.

In Chapter 2, *"A Unifying Framework for Robot Control with Redundant Degrees of Freedom"*, we present the general architecture which allows us to both understand motor skill representation and execution from an analytical point of view as well as it serves as the basis of our motor skill learning endeavours.

In Chapter 3, *"Learning Tracking Control in Operational Space"*, we focus on learning how to generate joint-space motor commands in order to achieve task-space tracking. While this chapter can be read separately from Chapter 2, it makes use of the main principle, i.e., the point-wise cost function. In this context, we present first the general EM-like

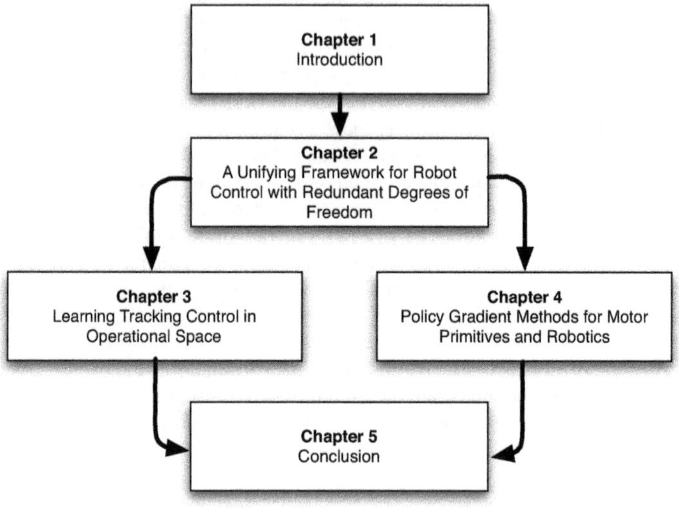

Figure 1.2: This figure illustrates the outline and relation of the book chapters.

algorithm for reinforcement learning and, subsequently, we derive the Reward-Weighted Regression algorithm from it.

While Chapters 3 and 2 assume given tasks in a differential form, Chapter 4, *"Policy Gradient Methods for Motor Primitives and Robotics"*, focusses on the learning and/or refinement of tasks represented by motor primitives. For achieving this, we compare reinforcement learning methods for parameterized policies with a strong bias towards high-dimensional systems such as robots and episodic task-learning. The best performing method, the Episodic Natural Actor-Critic is then shown to be efficient in task learning for an anthropomorphic robot.

Finally, in Chapter 5, *"Conclusion "*, we give a conclusion and discuss future work.

Chapter 2

A Unifying Framework for Robot Control with Redundant Degrees of Freedom

Theory attracts practice as the magnet attracts iron.
Carl Friedrich Gauss (German mathematician, 1777-1855)

One of the most important reasons why learning methods are not dominating the field of robotics yet is the depth of human insight into the structure and control of mechanical systems. Pure machine learning approaches which neglect the insights from analytical robotics often end up with ill-posed problems (e.g., learning inverse kinematics by supervised learning can result in inconsistent solutions), or with inferior solutions (e.g., the linear appearance of velocities and accelerations in differential kinematic models can be incorporated). Thus, this chapter attempts to make use of that knowledge in order to establish the theoretical basis for a machine learning framework for motor skills from an analytical dynamics point of view. The results presented in this chapter are a key ingredient for Chapter 3. They serve also as basis for the operational space control learning framework and they suggest a task learning approach based on motor primitive representations as discussed in Chapter 4.

Recently, Udwadia (2003) suggested to derive tracking controllers for mechanical systems with redundant degrees-of-freedom (DOFs) using a generalization of Gauss' principle of least constraint. This method allows reformulating control problems as a special class of point-wise optimal controllers. In this book chapter, we take this line of reasoning one step further and demonstrate that several well-known and also novel nonlinear robot control laws can be derived from this generic methodology. We show experimental verifications on a Sarcos Master Arm robot for some of the the derived controllers. The suggested approach offers a promising unification and simplification of nonlinear control law design for robots obeying rigid body dynamics equations, both with or without external constraints. It can be shown to generalize to hierarchical task prioritization frameworks, and, in a more limited case, it can be justified from the viewpoint of an infinite horizon point of view.

2.1 Introduction

The literature on robot control with redundant degrees-of-freedom (DOFs) has introduced many different approaches of how to resolve kinematic redundancy in complex robots and how to combine redundancy resolution with appriopriate control methods (e.g., see (Nakanishi, Cory, Mistry, Peters, & Schaal, 2005) for an overview). For instance, methods can be classified to operate out of velocity-based, acceleration-based, and force-based principles, they can focus on local or global redundancy resolution strategies (Baillieul & Martin, 1990), and they can have a variety of approaches how to include optimization criteria to maintain control in the null space of a movement task. When studying the different techniques, it sometimes appears that they were created from ingenious insights of the orginal researchers, but that there is also a missing thread that links different techniques to a common basic principle.

We follow Udwadia's (2003) suggestion to reinterpretate tracking control in terms of constrained mechanics, which was inspired by results from analytical dynamics with constrained motion. The major insight is that tracking control can be reformulated in terms of constraints, which in turn allows the application of a generalization of Gauss' principle of least constraint[1] (Udwadia & Kalaba, 1996; Bruyninckx & Khatib, 2000) to derive a control law. This insight leads to a specialized point-wise optimal control framework for controlled mechanical systems. While it is not applicable to non-mechanical control problems with arbitrary cost functions, it yields an important class of optimal controllers, i.e., the class where the problem requires task achievement under minimal squared motor commands with respect to a specified metric. In this book chapter, we develop this line of thinking one step further and show that it can be used as a general way of deriving robot controllers for systems with redundant DOFs, which offers a useful unification of several approaches in the literature. We discuss the necessary conditions for the stability of the controller in task space if the system can be modeled with sufficient precision and the chosen metric is appropriate. For assuring stability in configuration space further considerations may apply. To explore the feasibility of our framework and to demonstrate the effects of the weighting metric, we evaluate some of the derived controllers on an end-effector tracking task with an anthropomorphic robot arm.

This book chapter is organized as follows: firstly, a optimal control framework based on (Udwadia, 2003) is presented and analyzed. Secondly, we discuss different robot control problems in this framework including joint and task space tracking, force and hybrid control. We show how both established and novel controllers can be derived in a unified way. Finally, we evaluate some of these controllers on a Sarcos Master Arm robot.

[1]Gauss' principle of the least constraint (Udwadia & Kalaba, 1996) is a general axiom on the mechanics of constrained motions. It states that if a mechanical system is constrained by another mechanical structure the resulting acceleration $\ddot{\mathbf{x}}$ of the system will be such that it minimizes $(\ddot{\mathbf{x}} - \mathbf{M}^{-1}\mathbf{F})^T\mathbf{M}^{-1}(\ddot{\mathbf{x}} - \mathbf{M}^{-1}\mathbf{F})$ while fulfilling the constraint. Here $\mathbf{M}$ denotes the inertia matrix and $\mathbf{F}$ denotes the internal forces.

2.2 A Unifying Methodology for Robot Control

A variety of robot control problems can be motivated by the desire to achieve a task accurately while minimizing the squared motor commands, e.g., we intend to track a trajectory with minimum generated torques. Such problems can be formalized as a type of minimum effort control. In this section, we will show how the robot dynamics and the control problem can be brought into a general form which, subsequently, will allow us to compute the optimal control commands with respect to a desired metric. We will augment this framework such that we can ensure the necessary conditions for stability both in the joint space of the robot as well as in the task space of the problem.

2.2.1 Formulating Robot Control Problems

We assume the well-known rigid-body dynamics model of manipulator robotics with n degrees of freedom given by the equation

$$\mathbf{u} = \mathbf{M}(\mathbf{q})\ddot{\mathbf{q}} + \mathbf{C}(\mathbf{q}, \dot{\mathbf{q}}) + \mathbf{G}(\mathbf{q}), \tag{2.1}$$

where $\mathbf{u} \in \mathbb{R}^n$ is the vector of motor commands (i.e., torques or forces), $\mathbf{q}, \dot{\mathbf{q}}, \ddot{\mathbf{q}} \in \mathbb{R}^n$ are the vectors of joint position, velocities and acceleration, respectively, $\mathbf{M}(\mathbf{q}) \in \mathbb{R}^{n \times n}$ is the mass or inertia matrix, $\mathbf{C}(\mathbf{q}, \dot{\mathbf{q}}) \in \mathbb{R}^n$ denotes centripetal and Coriolis forces, and $\mathbf{G}(\mathbf{q}) \in \mathbb{R}^n$ denotes forces due to gravity (Yoshikawa, 1990; De Wit et al., 1996). At many points we will write the dynamics equations as $\mathbf{M}(\mathbf{q})\ddot{\mathbf{q}} = \mathbf{u}(\mathbf{q}, \dot{\mathbf{q}}) + \mathbf{F}(\mathbf{q}, \dot{\mathbf{q}})$ where $\mathbf{F}(\mathbf{q}, \dot{\mathbf{q}}) = -\mathbf{C}(\mathbf{q}, \dot{\mathbf{q}}) - \mathbf{G}(\mathbf{q})$ for notational convenience. We assume that a sufficiently accurate model of our robot system is available.

A task for the robot is assumed to be described in the form of a constraint, i.e., it is given by a function

$$\mathbf{h}(\mathbf{q}, \dot{\mathbf{q}}, t) = 0. \tag{2.2}$$

where $\mathbf{h} \in \mathbb{R}^k$ with an arbitrary dimensionality k. For example, if the robot is supposed to follow a desired trajectory $\mathbf{q}_{\text{des}}(t) \in \mathbb{R}^n$, we could formulate it by $\mathbf{h}(\mathbf{q}, \dot{\mathbf{q}}, t) = \mathbf{q} - \mathbf{q}_{\text{des}}(t) = 0$; this case is analyzed in detail in Section 2.3.1. The function h can be considered a task function in the sense of the framework proposed in (Samson, Borgne, & Espiau, 1991).

We consider only tasks where equation (2.2) can be reformulated as

$$\mathbf{A}(\mathbf{q}, \dot{\mathbf{q}}, t)\ddot{\mathbf{q}} = \mathbf{b}(\mathbf{q}, \dot{\mathbf{q}}, t), \tag{2.3}$$

which can be achieved for most tasks by differentiation of equation (2.2) with respect to time, assuming that h is sufficiently smooth. For example, our previous task, upon differentiation, becomes $\ddot{\mathbf{q}} = \ddot{\mathbf{q}}_{\text{des}}(t)$ so that $\mathbf{A} = \mathbf{I}$ and $\mathbf{b} = \ddot{\mathbf{q}}_{\text{des}}(t)$. An advantage of this task formulation is that non-holomonic constraints can be treated in the same general way.

In Section 2.3, we will give task descriptions first in the general form of Equation (2.2), and then derive the resulting controller, which is the linear in accelerations, as shown in Equation (2.3).

2.2.2 Point-wise Optimal Control Framework

Let us assume that we are given a robot model and a constraint formulation of the task as described in the previous section. In this case, we can characterize the desired properties of the framework as follows: first, the task has to be achieved perfectly, i.e., $h(\mathbf{q}, \dot{\mathbf{q}}, t) = 0$, or equivalently, $\mathbf{A}(\mathbf{q}, \dot{\mathbf{q}}, t)\ddot{\mathbf{q}} = \mathbf{b}(\mathbf{q}, \dot{\mathbf{q}}, t)$, holds at all times. Second, we intend to minimize the control command with respect to some given metric, i.e., $J(t) = \mathbf{u}^T\mathbf{N}(t)\mathbf{u}$, at *each* instant of time, with positive semi-definite matrix $\mathbf{N}(t)$. The solution to this point-wise optimal control problem (Spong, Thorp, & Kleinwaks, 1984, 1986) can be derived from a generalization of Gauss' principle, as originally suggested in (Udwadia, 2003). It is also a generalization of the propositions in (Udwadia & Kalaba, 1996; Bruyninckx & Khatib, 2000). We formalize this idea in the following proposition.

Proposition 2.1 *The class of controllers which minimizes*

$$J(t) = \mathbf{u}^T\mathbf{N}(t)\mathbf{u}, \tag{2.4}$$

for a mechanical system $\mathbf{M}(\mathbf{q})\ddot{\mathbf{q}} = \mathbf{u}(\mathbf{q}, \dot{\mathbf{q}}) + \mathbf{F}(\mathbf{q}, \dot{\mathbf{q}})$ *while fulfilling the task constraint*

$$\mathbf{A}(\mathbf{q}, \dot{\mathbf{q}}, t)\ddot{\mathbf{q}} = \mathbf{b}(\mathbf{q}, \dot{\mathbf{q}}, t), \tag{2.5}$$

is given by

$$\mathbf{u} = \mathbf{N}^{-1/2}(\mathbf{A}\mathbf{M}^{-1}\mathbf{N}^{-1/2})^{+}(\mathbf{b} - \mathbf{A}\mathbf{M}^{-1}\mathbf{F}), \tag{2.6}$$

where $\mathbf{D}^{+}$ *denotes the pseudo-inverse for a general matrix* $\mathbf{D}$*, and* $\mathbf{D}^{1/2}$ *denotes the symmetric, positive definite matrix for which* $\mathbf{D}^{1/2}\mathbf{D}^{1/2} = \mathbf{D}$.

Proof. By defining $\mathbf{z} = \mathbf{N}^{1/2}\mathbf{u} = \mathbf{N}^{1/2}(\mathbf{M}\ddot{\mathbf{q}} - \mathbf{F})$, we obtain the accelerations $\ddot{\mathbf{q}} = \mathbf{M}^{-1}\mathbf{N}^{-1/2}(\mathbf{z} + \mathbf{N}^{1/2}\mathbf{F})$. Since the task constraint $\mathbf{A}\ddot{\mathbf{q}} = \mathbf{b}$ has to be fulfilled, we have

$$\mathbf{A}\mathbf{M}^{-1}\mathbf{N}^{-1/2}\mathbf{z} = \mathbf{b} - \mathbf{A}\mathbf{M}^{-1}\mathbf{F}. \tag{2.7}$$

The vector $\mathbf{z}$ which minimizes $J(t) = \mathbf{z}^T\mathbf{z}$ while fulfilling Equation (2.7), is given by $\mathbf{z} = (\mathbf{A}\mathbf{M}^{-1}\mathbf{N}^{-1/2})^{+}(\mathbf{b} - \mathbf{A}\mathbf{M}^{-1}\mathbf{F})$, and as the motor command is given by $\mathbf{u} = \mathbf{N}^{-1/2}\mathbf{z}$, the proposition holds. ∎

The choice of the metric $\mathbf{N}$ plays a central role as it determines how the control effort is distributed over the joints. Often, we require a solution which has a kinematic interpretation; such a solution is usually given by a metric like $\mathbf{N} = (\mathbf{M} \cdot \mathbf{M})^{-1} = \mathbf{M}^{-2}$. In other cases, the control force $\mathbf{u}$ may be required to comply with the principle of virtual displacements by d'Alembert for which the metric $\mathbf{N} = \mathbf{M}^{-1}$ is more appropriate

(Udwadia & Kalaba, 1996; Bruyninckx & Khatib, 2000). In practical cases, one would want to distribute the forces such that joints with stronger motors get a higher workload which can also be achieved by a metric such as $\mathbf{N} = \mathrm{diag}(\hat{\tau}_1^{-2}, \hat{\tau}_2^{-2}, \ldots, \hat{\tau}_n^{-2})$ where the nominal torques $\hat{\tau}_i$ are used for the appropriate distribution of the motor commands. In Section 2.3, we will see how the choice of $\mathbf{N}$ results in several different controllers.

2.2.3 Necessary Conditions for Stability

Up to this point, this framework has been introduced in an idealized fashion neglecting the possibility of imperfect initial conditions and measurement noise. Therefore, we modify our approach slightly for ensuring stability. However, the stability of this framework as well as most related approaches derivable form this framework cannot be shown conclusively but only in special cases (Hsu, Hauser, & Sastry, 1989; Arimoto, 1996). Therefore, we can only outline the necessary conditions for stability, i.e., (i) the achievement of the task which will be achieved through a modification of the framework in Section 2.2.3.1 and (ii) the prevention of undesired side-effects in joint-space. The later are a result of under-constrained tasks, i.e., tasks where some degrees of freedom of the robot are redundant for task achievements, can cause undesired postures or even instability in joint-space. This problem will be treated in Section 2.2.3.2.

2.2.3.1 Task Achievement

Up to this point, we have assumed that we always have perfect initial conditions, i.e., that the robot fulfills the constraint in Equation (2.3) at startup, and that we know the robot model perfectly. Here, we treat deviations to these assumptions as disturbances and add means of disturbance rejection to our framework. This disturbance rejection can be achieved by requiring that the desired task is an attractor, e.g., it could be prescribed as a dynamical system in the form

$$\dot{\mathbf{h}}(\mathbf{q}, \dot{\mathbf{q}}, t) = \mathbf{f}_{\mathbf{h}}(\mathbf{h}, t), \tag{2.8}$$

where $\mathbf{h} = 0$ is a globally asymptotically stable equilibrium point – or a locally asymptotically stable equilibrium point with a sufficiently large region of attraction. Note that $\mathbf{h}$ can be a function of robot variables (as in end-effector trajectory control in Section 2.3.2) but often it suffices to choose it as a function of the state vector (for example for joint-space trajectory control as in Section 2.3.1). In the case of holonomic tasks (such as tracking control for a robot arm), i.e. $h_i(\mathbf{q}, t) = 0, i = 1, 2, \ldots, k$ we can make use of a particularly simple form and turn this task into an attractor

$$\ddot{h}_i + \delta_i \dot{h}_i + \kappa_i h = 0, \tag{2.9}$$

where δ_i and κ_i are chosen appropriately. We will make use of this 'trick' in order to derive several algorithms. Obviously, different attractors with more desirable convergence

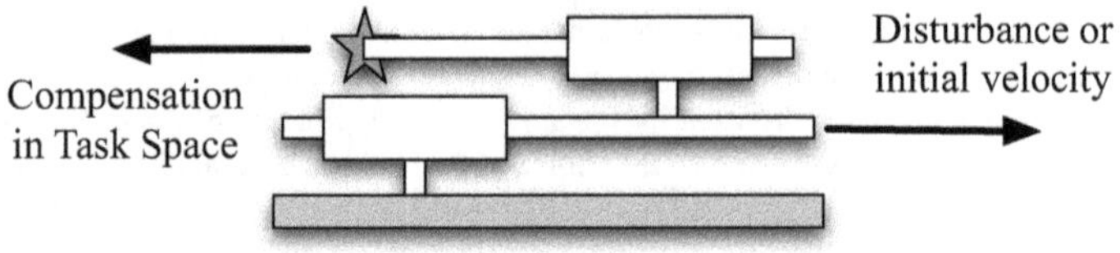

Figure 2.1: In the presence of disturbances or non-zero initial conditions, stable task dynamics will not result in joint-space stability.

properties (and/or larger basins of attraction) can be obtained by choosing $\mathbf{f}_h$ appropriately.

If we have such task-space stabilization, we can assure that the control law will achieve the task at least in a region near to the desired trajectory. We demonstrate this issue in the following proposition.

Proposition 2.2 *If we can assure the attractor property of the task* $\mathbf{h}(\mathbf{q}, \dot{\mathbf{q}}, t) = 0$, *or equivalently,* $\mathbf{A}(\mathbf{q}, \dot{\mathbf{q}}, t)\ddot{\mathbf{q}} = \mathbf{b}(\mathbf{q}, \dot{\mathbf{q}}, t)$, *and if our robot model is accurate, the optimal controller of Equation (2.6) will achieve the task asymptotically.*

Proof. When combining the robot dynamics equation with the controller, and after reordering the terms, we obtain

$$\mathbf{AM}^{-1}(\mathbf{M}\ddot{\mathbf{q}} - \mathbf{F}) = (\mathbf{AM}^{-1}\mathbf{N}^{-1/2})^{+}(\mathbf{b} - \mathbf{AM}^{-1}\mathbf{F}). \quad (2.10)$$

If we now premultiply the equation with $\mathbf{D} = \mathbf{AM}^{-1}\mathbf{N}^{-1/2}$, and noting that $\mathbf{DD}^{+}\mathbf{D} = \mathbf{D}$, we obtain $\mathbf{A}\ddot{\mathbf{q}} = \mathbf{DD}^{+}\mathbf{b} = \mathbf{b}$. The equality follows because the original trajectory defined by $\mathbf{A}\ddot{\mathbf{q}} = \mathbf{b}$ yields a consistent set of equations. If this equation describes an attractor, we will have asymptotically perfect task achievement. ∎

In some cases, such as joint trajectory tracking control discussed in Section 2.3.1, Proposition 2.2 will suffice for a stability proof in a Lyapunov sense (Yoshikawa, 1990; De Wit et al., 1996). However, for certain tasks such as end-effector tracking control discussed in Section 2.3.1, this is not the case and stability can only be assured in special cases (Hsu et al., 1989; Arimoto, 1996).

2.2.3.2 Prevention of Control Problems in Joint-Space

Even if stability in task space can be shown, it is not immediately clear whether the control law is stable in joint-space. Example 2.1, illustrates a problematic situation where a redundant robot arm achieves an end-effector tracking task and is provably stable in task-space, but nevertheless also provably *unstable in joint-space.*

Example 2.1 *Let us assume a simple prismatic robot with two horizontal, parallel links as illustrated in Figure 2.1. The mass matrix of this robot is a constant given by* $\mathbf{M} = \mathrm{diag}(m_1, 0) + m_2\mathbf{1}$ *where* $\mathbf{1}$ *denotes a matrix having only ones as entries, and the additional forces are* $\mathbf{F} = \mathbf{C} + \mathbf{G} = \mathbf{0}$*. Let us assume the task is to move the end-effector* $x = q_1 + q_2$ *along a desired position* x_{des}*, i.e., the task can be specified by* $\mathbf{A} = [1, 1]$*, and* $b = \ddot{x}_{des} + \delta(\dot{x}_{des} - \dot{x}) + \kappa(x_{des} - x)$ *after double differentiation and task stabilization. While the task dynamics are obviously stable (which can be verified using the constant Eigenvalues of the system), the initial condition* $q_1(t_0) = x_{des}(t_0) - q_2(t_0)$ *would result in both* $q_i(t)$*'s diverging into opposite directions for any non-zero initial velocities or in the presence of disturbances for arbitrary initial conditions. The reason for this behavior is obvious: the effort of stabilizing in joint space is not task relevant and would increase the cost.*

While this example is similar to problems with non-minimum phase nonlinear control systems (Isidori, 1995)), the problems encountered are not the failure of the task controller, but rather due to internal dynamics, e.g., hitting of joint limits. From this example, we see that the basic general framework of contrained mechanics does not always suffice to derive useful control laws, and that it has to be augmented to incorporate joint stabilization for the robot without affecting the task achievement. One possibility is to introduce a joint-space motor command $\mathbf{u}_1$ as an additional component of the the motor command $\mathbf{u}$, i.e.,

$$\mathbf{u} = \mathbf{u}_1 + \mathbf{u}_2(\mathbf{u}_1), \tag{2.11}$$

where the first component $\mathbf{u}_1$ denotes an arbitrary joint-space motor command for stabilization, while the second component $\mathbf{u}_2(\mathbf{u}_1)$ denotes the task-space motor command generated with the previously explained equations. The task-space component depends on the joint-space component as it has to compensate for it in the range of the task space. We can show that task achievement $\mathbf{A}\ddot{\mathbf{q}} = \mathbf{b}$ by the controller is not affected by the choice of the joint-space control law $\mathbf{u}_1$.

Proposition 2.3 *For any chosen joint stabilizing control law* $\mathbf{u}_1 = f(\mathbf{q})$*, the resulting task space control law* $\mathbf{u}_2(\mathbf{u}_1)$ *ensures that the joint-space stabilization acts in the null-space of the task achievement.*

Proof. When determining $\mathbf{u}_2$, we consider $\mathbf{u}_1$ to be part of our additional forces in the rigid body dynamics, i.e., we have $\tilde{\mathbf{F}} = \mathbf{F} + \mathbf{u}_1$. We obtain $\mathbf{u}_2 = \mathbf{N}^{-1/2}(\mathbf{A}\mathbf{M}^{-1}\mathbf{N}^{-1/2})^{+}(\mathbf{b} - \mathbf{A}\mathbf{M}^{-1}\tilde{\mathbf{F}})$ using Proposition 2.1. By reordering the complete control law $\mathbf{u} = \mathbf{u}_1 + \mathbf{u}_2(\mathbf{u}_1)$, we obtain

$$\begin{aligned} \mathbf{u} &= \mathbf{u}_1 + \mathbf{N}^{-1/2}(\mathbf{A}\mathbf{M}^{-1}\mathbf{N}^{-1/2})^{+}(\mathbf{b} - \mathbf{A}\mathbf{M}^{-1}(\mathbf{F} + \mathbf{u}_1)), \\ &= \mathbf{N}^{-1/2}(\mathbf{A}\mathbf{M}^{-1}\mathbf{N}^{-1/2})^{+}(\mathbf{b} - \mathbf{A}\mathbf{M}^{-1}\mathbf{F}) \\ &+ \left[\mathbf{I} - \mathbf{N}^{-1/2}(\mathbf{A}\mathbf{M}^{-1}\mathbf{N}^{-1/2})^{+}\mathbf{A}\mathbf{M}^{-1}\right]\mathbf{u}_1, \\ &= \mathbf{N}^{-1/2}(\mathbf{A}\mathbf{M}^{-1}\mathbf{N}^{-1/2})^{+}(\mathbf{b} - \mathbf{A}\mathbf{M}^{-1}\mathbf{F}) \end{aligned} \tag{2.12}$$

$$+\mathbf{N}^{-1/2}\left[\mathbf{I}-(\mathbf{A}\mathbf{M}^{-1}\mathbf{N}^{-1/2})^{+}(\mathbf{A}\mathbf{M}^{-1}\mathbf{N}^{-1/2})\right]\mathbf{N}^{1/2}\mathbf{u}_1,$$

The task space is defined by $\mathbf{N}^{-1/2}(\mathbf{A}\mathbf{M}^{-1}\mathbf{N}^{-1/2})^{+}$, and the projection matrix given by $\mathbf{N}^{-1/2}\left[\mathbf{I}-(\mathbf{A}\mathbf{M}^{-1}\mathbf{N}^{-1/2})^{+}(\mathbf{A}\mathbf{M}^{-1}\mathbf{N}^{-1/2})\right]$ ensures that the joint-space control law and the task space control law are $\mathbf{N}$-orthogonal, i.e., the task accomplishment is independent of the joint-space stabilization. ■

Despite that the task is still achieved, the optimal control problem is affected by the restructuring of our control law. While we originally minimized $J(t) = \mathbf{u}^T\mathbf{N}(t)\mathbf{u}$, we now have a modified cost function

$$\tilde{J}(t) = \mathbf{u}_2^T\mathbf{N}(t)\mathbf{u}_2 = (\mathbf{u}-\mathbf{u}_1)^T\mathbf{N}(t)(\mathbf{u}-\mathbf{u}_1), \tag{2.13}$$

which is equivalent to stating that the complete control law $\mathbf{u}$ should be as close to the joint-space control law $\mathbf{u}_1$ as possible under task achievement.

This reformulation can have significant advantages if used appropriately. For example, in a variety of applications – such as using the robot as a haptic interface – a compensation of the robot's gravitational, coriolis and centripetal forces in joint space can be useful. Such a compensation can only be derived when making use of the modified control law. In this case, we set $\mathbf{u}_1 = -\mathbf{F} = \mathbf{C}+\mathbf{G}$, which allows us to obtain

$$\mathbf{u}_2 = \mathbf{N}^{-1/2}(\mathbf{A}\mathbf{M}^{-1}\mathbf{N}^{-1/2})^{+}\mathbf{b}, \tag{2.14}$$

which does not contain these forces, and we would have a complete control law of $\mathbf{u} = \mathbf{C}+\mathbf{G}+\mathbf{N}^{-1/2}(\mathbf{A}\mathbf{M}^{-1}\mathbf{N}^{-1/2})^{+}\mathbf{b}$.

2.2.4 Hierachical Extension

In high-dimensional systems with complex applications, we can often have a large number of tasks, $\mathbf{A}_1\ddot{\mathbf{q}} = \mathbf{b}_1$, $\mathbf{A}_2\ddot{\mathbf{q}} = \mathbf{b}_2$, ..., $\mathbf{A}_n\ddot{\mathbf{q}} = \mathbf{b}_n$ that have to be accomplished in parallel. These tasks often partially conflict, e.g., when the number of tasks exceeds the number of degrees of freedom or some of these tasks cannot be achieved in combination with each other. Therefore, the combination of these tasks into a single large task is not always practical and, instead, the tasks need prioritization, e.g., the higher the number of the task, the higher its priority. Task prioritized control solutions have been discussed in the literature (Nakamura, Hanafusa, & Yoshikawa, 1987; Hollerbach & Suh, 1987; Maciejewski & Klein, 1985; Hanafusa, Yoshikawa, & Nakamura, 1981; Yamane & Nakamura, 2003; Sentis & Khatib, 2004; Siciliano & Slotine, 1991; Khatib, Sentis, Park, & Warren, 2004; Sentis & Khatib, 2005). Most previous approaches were kinematic and discussed only a small, fixed number of tasks; to our knowledge, (Sentis & Khatib, 2004, 2005) were among the first to discuss arbitrary task numbers and dynamical decoupling, i.e., a different metric from our point of view. The proposed framework allows the generalization for arbitrary metrics and more general problems as will be shown in Proposition 2.3. The prioritized motor command is given by

$$\mathbf{u} = \mathbf{u}_1 + \mathbf{u}_2(\mathbf{u}_1) + \mathbf{u}_3(\mathbf{u}_1 + \mathbf{u}_2) + \ldots + \mathbf{u}_n(\mathbf{u}_1 + \ldots + \mathbf{u}_{n-1}), \tag{2.15}$$

where $\mathbf{u}_n(\mathbf{u}_1 + \ldots + \mathbf{u}_{n-1})$ is the highest-priority control law as a function of the lower level $\mathbf{u}_1, \ldots, \mathbf{u}_{n-1}$ and cancels out all influence $\mathbf{u}_1 + \ldots + \mathbf{u}_{n-1}$ which prohibit the execution of its task. The motor commands for each degree of freedom can be given by the following Proposition:

Proposition 2.4 *A set of hierachically prioritized constraints* $\mathbf{A}_i\ddot{\mathbf{q}} = \mathbf{b}_i$ *where the priority is represented by* $i = 1, 2, \ldots, n$ *(here, a higher number idenotes a higher priority) can be controlled by*

$$\mathbf{u} = \mathbf{u}_1 + \sum_{i=2}^{n} \mathbf{u}_i\left(\sum\nolimits_{k=1}^{i-1} \mathbf{u}_k\right), \tag{2.16}$$

where $\mathbf{u}_i(\mathbf{u}_\Sigma) = \mathbf{N}^{-1/2}(\mathbf{A}_i\mathbf{M}^{-1}\mathbf{N}^{-1/2})^{+}(\mathbf{b} - \mathbf{A}_i\mathbf{M}^{-1}(\mathbf{F} + \mathbf{u}_\Sigma))$. *For any* $k < i$, *the lower-priority control law* $\mathbf{u}_k$ *acts in the null-space of the higher-priority control law* $\mathbf{u}_i$ *and any higher-priority control law* $\mathbf{u}_i$ *cancels all parts of the lower-priority control law* $\mathbf{u}_k$ *which conflict with its task achievement.*

Proof. We first simply create the control laws $\mathbf{u}_1$ and $\mathbf{u}_2(\mathbf{u}_1)$ as described before and then make use of Proposition 2.3, which proves that this approach is correct for $n = 2$. Let us assume now that it is true for $n = m$. In this case, we can consider $\tilde{\mathbf{u}}_1 = \mathbf{u}_1 + \mathbf{u}_2 + \ldots + \mathbf{u}_m$ our joint-space control law and $\tilde{\mathbf{u}}_2 = \mathbf{u}_{m+1}$ the task-space control law. If we now make use of Proposition 2.3 again, we realize that $\tilde{\mathbf{u}}_1 = \mathbf{u}_1 + \mathbf{u}_2 + \ldots + \mathbf{u}_m$ acts in the null-space of $\tilde{\mathbf{u}}_2 = \mathbf{u}_{m+1}$ and that all components of $\mathbf{u}_1, \mathbf{u}_2, \ldots, \mathbf{u}_m$ which conflict with $\mathbf{u}_{m+1}$ will be canceled out. Therefore, the proposition also remains true for $n = m + 1$. This proves the proposition by induction. ■

From the viewpoint of optimization, the control laws obtained in Proposition 2.4 have a straightforward interpretation like the combination of joint and task-space control laws: each subsequent control law is chosen so that the control effort deviates minimally from the effort created from the previous control laws.

Example 2.2 *Robot locomotion is a straightforward example for such an approach. Traditionally, all tasks are often meshed into one big tasks (Pratt & Pratt, 1998). However, the most essential task is the balancing of the robot to prevent accidents; it can, for instance, be achieved by a balancing task* $\mathbf{A}_3\ddot{\mathbf{q}} = \mathbf{b}_3$ *similar to a spring-damper system pulling the system to an upright position. Additionally, the center of the torso should follow a desired trajectory – unless the desired path would make the robot fall. This gait generating task would be given by* $\mathbf{A}_2\ddot{\mathbf{q}} = \mathbf{b}_2$. *Additionally, we want to have joint-space stability as the unconstrained degrees of freedom such as the arms might otherwise move all the time. The joint-space stabilization can be expressed as a constraint*

$\mathbf{A}_1\ddot{\mathbf{q}} = \mathbf{b}_1$ *pulling the robot towards a rest posture. The combined motor command is now given by* $\mathbf{u} = \mathbf{u}_1 + \mathbf{u}_2(\mathbf{u}_1) + \mathbf{u}_3(\mathbf{u}_1 + \mathbf{u}_2)$ *with the single control laws are obtained by* $\mathbf{u}_i(\mathbf{u}_\Sigma) = \mathbf{N}^{-1/2}(\mathbf{A}_i\mathbf{M}^{-1}\mathbf{N}^{-1/2})^{+}(\mathbf{b} - \mathbf{A}_i\mathbf{M}^{-1}(\mathbf{F} + \mathbf{u}_\Sigma))$ *with* $i = 1, 2, 3$.

Ideas similar to Example 2.2 have been explored in (Yamane & Nakamura, 2003; Sentis & Khatib, 2004; Khatib et al., 2004; Sentis & Khatib, 2005) and we are currently working on applying this framework to locomotion similar to Example 2.2.

2.3 Robot Control Laws

The previously described framework offers a variety of applications in robotics – we will only focus on some the most important ones in this book chapter. Most of these controllers which we will derive are known from the literature, but often from very different, and sometimes convoluted, building principles. In this section, we show how a large variety of control laws for different situations can be derived in a simple and straightforward way by using the unifying framework that has been developed hereto. We derive control laws for joint-space trajectory control for both fully actuated and overactuated "muscle-like" robot systems from our framework. We also discuss task-space tracking control systems, and show that most well-known inverse kinematics controllers are applications of the same principle. Additionally, we will discuss how the control of constrained manipulators through impedance and hybrid control can be easily handled within our framework.

2.3.1 Joint-Space Trajectory Control

The first control problem we address is joint-space trajectory control. We consider two different situations: (a) We control a fully actuated robot arm in joint-space, and (b) we control an overactuated arm. The case (b) could, for example, have agonist-antagonist muscles as actuators similar to a human arm[2].

2.3.1.1 Fully Actuated Robot

The first case which we consider is the one of a robot arm which is actuated at every degree of freedom. We have the trajectory as constraint with $\mathbf{h}(\mathbf{q}, t) = \mathbf{q}(t) - \mathbf{q}_d(t) = 0$. We turn this constraint into an attractor constraint using the idea in Section 2.2.3.1, yielding

$$(\ddot{\mathbf{q}} - \ddot{\mathbf{q}}_d) + \mathbf{K}_D(\dot{\mathbf{q}} - \dot{\mathbf{q}}_d) + \mathbf{K}_P(\mathbf{q} - \mathbf{q}_d) = 0, \tag{2.17}$$

where $\mathbf{K}_D$ are positive-definite damping gains, and $\mathbf{K}_P$ are positive-definite proportional gains. We can bring this constraint into the form $\mathbf{A}(\mathbf{q}, \dot{\mathbf{q}})\ddot{\mathbf{q}} = \mathbf{b}(\mathbf{q}, \dot{\mathbf{q}})$ with

$$\mathbf{A} = \mathbf{I}, \tag{2.18}$$

[2]An open topic of interest is to handle underactuated control systems. This will be part of future work.

$$\mathbf{b} = \ddot{\mathbf{q}}_d + \mathbf{K}_D(\dot{\mathbf{q}}_d - \dot{\mathbf{q}}) - \mathbf{K}_P(\mathbf{q}_d - \mathbf{q}). \tag{2.19}$$

Proposition 2.1 can be used to derive the controller. Using $(\mathbf{M}^{-1}\mathbf{N}^{-1/2})^{+} = \mathbf{N}^{1/2}\mathbf{M}$ as both matrices are of full rank, we obtain

$$\begin{aligned}\mathbf{u} &= \mathbf{u}_1 + \mathbf{N}^{-1/2}(\mathbf{A}\mathbf{M}^{-1}\mathbf{N}^{-1/2})^{+}(\mathbf{b} - \mathbf{A}\mathbf{M}^{-1}(\mathbf{F} + \mathbf{u}_1)),\\ &= \mathbf{M}(\ddot{\mathbf{q}}_d + \mathbf{K}_D(\dot{\mathbf{q}}_d - \dot{\mathbf{q}}) + \mathbf{K}_P(\mathbf{q}_d - \mathbf{q})) + \mathbf{C} + \mathbf{G}. \end{aligned} \tag{2.20}$$

Note that – not surprisingly – all joint-space motor commands or virtual forces $\mathbf{u}_1$ always disappear from the control law and that the chosen metric $\mathbf{N}$ is not relevant – the derived solution is unique and general. This equation is a well-known text book control law, i.e., the **Inverse Dynamics Control Law** (Yoshikawa, 1990; De Wit et al., 1996).

2.3.1.2 Overactuated Robots

Overactuated robots, as they can be found in biological systems, are inherently different from the previously discussed robots. For instance, these systems are actuated by several linear actuators, e.g., muscles that often act on the system in form of opposing pairs. The interactions of the actuators can be modeled using the dynamics equations of

$$\mathbf{D}\mathbf{u} = \mathbf{M}(\mathbf{q})\ddot{\mathbf{q}} + \mathbf{C}(\mathbf{q}, \dot{\mathbf{q}}) + \mathbf{G}(\mathbf{q}), \tag{2.21}$$

where $\mathbf{D}$ depends on the geometric arrangement of the actuators. In the simple model of a two degree-of-freedom robot with antagonistic muscle-like activation, it would be given by

$$\mathbf{D} = \begin{bmatrix} -l & +l & 0 & 0 \\ 0 & 0 & -l & +l \end{bmatrix}, \tag{2.22}$$

where size of the entries $\mathbf{D}_{ij}$ denotes the moment arm length l_i and the sign of $\mathbf{D}_{ij}$ whether its agonist ($\mathbf{D}_{ij} > 0$) or antagonist muscle ($\mathbf{D}_{ij} < 0$). We can bring this equation into the standard form by multiplying it with $\mathbf{D}^{+}$, which results in a modified system where $\tilde{\mathbf{M}}(\mathbf{q}) = \mathbf{D}^{+}\mathbf{M}(\mathbf{q})$, and $\tilde{\mathbf{F}}(\mathbf{q}, \dot{\mathbf{q}}) = -\mathbf{D}^{+}\mathbf{C}(\mathbf{q}, \dot{\mathbf{q}}) - \mathbf{D}^{+}\mathbf{G}(\mathbf{q})$. If we express the desired trajectory as in the previous examples, we obtain the following controller

$$\mathbf{u} = \tilde{\mathbf{M}}^{1/2}(\mathbf{A}\tilde{\mathbf{M}}^{-1/2})^{+}(\mathbf{b} - \mathbf{A}\tilde{\mathbf{M}}^{-1}\tilde{\mathbf{F}}), \tag{2.23}$$

$$= \mathbf{D}^{+}\mathbf{M}(\ddot{\mathbf{q}}_d + \mathbf{K}_D(\dot{\mathbf{q}}_d - \dot{\mathbf{q}}) - \mathbf{K}_P(\mathbf{q}_d - \mathbf{q})) + \mathbf{D}^{+}(\mathbf{C} + \mathbf{G}). \tag{2.24}$$

While immediately intuitive, it noteworthy that this particular controller falls out of the presented framework in an natural way. It is straightforward to extend Proposition 2.1 to show that this is the constrained optimal solution to $J(t) = \mathbf{u}^T\mathbf{D}\mathbf{N}(t)\mathbf{D}\mathbf{u}$ at any instant of time.

2.3.2 End-effector Trajectory Control

While joint-space control of a trajectory $\mathbf{q}(t)$ is straightforward and the presented methodology appears to simply repeat earlier results from the literature – although derived from a different and unified perspective – the same cannot be said about end-effector control where the goal is to control the position $\mathbf{x}(t)$ of the end-effector. This problem is generically more difficult as the choice of the metric $\mathbf{N}$ determines the type of the resulting controller in an important way, and as the joint-space of the robot often has redundant degrees of freedom resulting in problems as already presented in Example 2.1. In the following, we will show how to derive different approaches to end-effector control from the presented framework, which will yield both established as well as novel control laws.

The task description is given by the end-effector trajectory acting as a constraint with $\mathbf{h}(\mathbf{q}, t) = \mathbf{f}(\mathbf{q}(t)) - \mathbf{x}_d(t) = \mathbf{x}(t) - \mathbf{x}_d(t) = \mathbf{0}$, where $\mathbf{x} = \mathbf{f}(\mathbf{q})$ denotes the forward kinematics. We turn this constraint into an attractor constraint using the idea in Section 2.2.3.1, yielding

$$(\ddot{\mathbf{x}} - \ddot{\mathbf{x}}_d) + \mathbf{K}_D(\dot{\mathbf{x}} - \dot{\mathbf{x}}_d) + \mathbf{K}_P(\mathbf{x} - \mathbf{x}_d) = 0, \tag{2.25}$$

where $\mathbf{K}_D$ are positive-definite damping gains, and $\mathbf{K}_P$ are positive-definite proportional gains. We make use of the differential forward kinematics, i.e.,

$$\dot{\mathbf{x}} = \mathbf{J}(\mathbf{q})\dot{\mathbf{q}}, \tag{2.26}$$

$$\ddot{\mathbf{x}} = \mathbf{J}(\mathbf{q})\ddot{\mathbf{q}} + \dot{\mathbf{J}}(\mathbf{q})\dot{\mathbf{q}}. \tag{2.27}$$

These equations allow us to formulate the problem in form of constraints, i.e., we intend to fulfill

$$\ddot{\mathbf{x}}_d + \mathbf{K}_D(\dot{\mathbf{x}}_d - \dot{\mathbf{x}}) + \mathbf{K}_P(\mathbf{x}_d - \mathbf{x}) = \mathbf{J}\ddot{\mathbf{q}} + \dot{\mathbf{J}}\dot{\mathbf{q}}, \tag{2.28}$$

and we can bring this equation into the form $\mathbf{A}(\mathbf{q}, \dot{\mathbf{q}})\ddot{\mathbf{q}} = \mathbf{b}(\mathbf{q}, \dot{\mathbf{q}})$ with

$$\mathbf{A}(\mathbf{q}, \dot{\mathbf{q}}) = \mathbf{J}, \tag{2.29}$$

$$\mathbf{b}(\mathbf{q}, \dot{\mathbf{q}}) = \ddot{\mathbf{x}}_d + \mathbf{K}_D(\dot{\mathbf{x}}_d - \dot{\mathbf{x}}) + \mathbf{K}_P(\mathbf{x}_d - \mathbf{x}) - \dot{\mathbf{J}}\dot{\mathbf{q}}. \tag{2.30}$$

These equations determine our task constraints. As long as the robot is not redundant $\mathbf{J}$ is invertible and similar to joint-space control, we will have one unique control law. However, when $\mathbf{J}$ is not uniquely invertible the resulting controller depends on the chosen metric and joint-space control law.

2.3.2.1 Separation of Kinematics and Dynamics Control

The choice of the metric $\mathbf{N}$ determines the nature of the controller. A metric of particular importance is $\mathbf{N} = \mathbf{M}^{-2}$ as this metric allows the decoupling of kinematics and dynamics control as we will see in this section. Using this metric in Proposition 2.1, we obtain a control law

$$\begin{aligned}\mathbf{u} &= \mathbf{u}_1 + \mathbf{N}^{-1/2}(\mathbf{A}\mathbf{M}^{-1}\mathbf{N}^{-1/2})^{+}(\mathbf{b} - \mathbf{A}\mathbf{M}^{-1}(\mathbf{F} + \mathbf{u}_1)),\\ &= \mathbf{M}\mathbf{J}^{+}(\ddot{\mathbf{x}}_d + \mathbf{K}_D(\dot{\mathbf{x}}_d - \dot{\mathbf{x}}) + \mathbf{K}_P(\mathbf{x}_d - \mathbf{x}) - \dot{\mathbf{J}}\dot{\mathbf{q}}) \\ &+ \mathbf{M}(\mathbf{I} - \mathbf{J}^{+}\mathbf{J})\mathbf{M}^{-1}\mathbf{u}_1 - \mathbf{M}\mathbf{J}^{+}\mathbf{J}\mathbf{M}^{-1}\mathbf{F}.\end{aligned} \tag{2.31}$$

If we choose the joint-space control law $\mathbf{u}_1 = \mathbf{u}_0 - \mathbf{F}$, we obtain the control law

$$\begin{aligned}\mathbf{u} &= \mathbf{M}\mathbf{J}^{+}(\ddot{\mathbf{x}}_d + \mathbf{K}_D(\dot{\mathbf{x}}_d - \dot{\mathbf{x}}) + \mathbf{K}_P(\mathbf{x}_d - \mathbf{x}) - \dot{\mathbf{J}}\dot{\mathbf{q}}) \\ &+ \mathbf{M}(\mathbf{I} - \mathbf{J}^{+}\mathbf{J})\mathbf{M}^{-1}\mathbf{u}_0 + \mathbf{C} + \mathbf{G}.\end{aligned} \tag{2.32}$$

This control law is the combination of a **resolved-acceleration kinematic controller** (Yoshikawa, 1990; Hsu et al., 1989) with a model-based controller and an additional null-space term. Often, $\mathbf{M}^{-1}\mathbf{u}_0$ is replaced by a desired acceleration term for the null-space stabilization. Similar controllers have been introduced in (Park, Chung, & Youm, 2002, 1995; Chung, Chung, & Y.Youm, 1993; K.C.Suh & Hollerbach, 1987). The null-space term can be eliminated by setting $\mathbf{u}_0 = \mathbf{0}$; however, this can result in instabilities if there are redundant degrees of freedom. This controller will be evaluated in Section 2.4.

2.3.2.2 Dynamically Consistent Decoupling

As noted earlier, another important metric is $\mathbf{N} = \mathbf{M}^{-1}$ as it is consistent with the principle of d'Alembert, i.e., the resulting control force can be re-interpreted as mechanical structures (e.g., springs and dampers) attached to the end-effector; it is therefore called dynamically consistent. Again, we use Proposition 2.1, and by defining $\tilde{\mathbf{F}} = \mathbf{F} + \mathbf{u}_1$ obtain the control law

$$\begin{aligned}\mathbf{u} &= \mathbf{u}_1 + \mathbf{N}^{-1/2}(\mathbf{A}\mathbf{M}^{-1}\mathbf{N}^{-1/2})^{+}(\mathbf{b} - \mathbf{A}\mathbf{M}^{-1}\tilde{\mathbf{F}}),\\ &= \mathbf{u}_1 + \mathbf{M}^{1/2}(\mathbf{J}\mathbf{M}^{-1/2})^{T}(\mathbf{J}\mathbf{M}^{-1}\mathbf{J}^{T})^{-1}(\mathbf{b} - \mathbf{J}\mathbf{M}^{-1}\tilde{\mathbf{F}}),\\ &= \mathbf{u}_1 + \mathbf{J}^{T}(\mathbf{J}\mathbf{M}^{-1}\mathbf{J}^{T})^{-1}(\mathbf{b} - \mathbf{J}\mathbf{M}^{-1}\tilde{\mathbf{F}}),\\ &= \mathbf{J}^{T}(\mathbf{J}\mathbf{M}^{-1}\mathbf{J}^{T})^{-1}(\ddot{\mathbf{x}}_d + \mathbf{K}_D(\dot{\mathbf{x}}_d - \dot{\mathbf{x}}) + \mathbf{K}_P(\mathbf{x}_d - \mathbf{x}) - \dot{\mathbf{J}}(\mathbf{q})\dot{\mathbf{q}}\\ &+ \mathbf{J}\mathbf{M}^{-1}(\mathbf{C} + \mathbf{G})) + \mathbf{M}(\mathbf{I} - \mathbf{M}^{-1}\mathbf{J}^{T}(\mathbf{J}\mathbf{M}^{-1}\mathbf{J}^{T})^{-1}\mathbf{J})\mathbf{M}^{-1}\mathbf{u}_1.\end{aligned}$$

It turns out that this is another well-known control law suggest in (Khatib, 1987) with an additional null-space term. This control-law is especially interesting as it has a clear physical interpretation (Udwadia & Kalaba, 1996; Bruyninckx & Khatib, 2000; Udwadia, 2003): the metric used is consistent with principle of virtual work of d'Alembert.

Similarly as before we can compensate for coriolis, centrifugal and gravitational forces in joint-space, i.e., setting $\mathbf{u}_1 = \mathbf{C} + \mathbf{G} + \mathbf{u}_0$. This yields a control law of

$$\mathbf{u} = \mathbf{J}^T(\mathbf{J}\mathbf{M}^{-1}\mathbf{J}^T)^{-1}(\ddot{\mathbf{x}}_d + \mathbf{K}_D(\dot{\mathbf{x}}_d - \dot{\mathbf{x}}) + \mathbf{K}_P(\mathbf{x}_d - \mathbf{x}) - \dot{\mathbf{J}}(\mathbf{q})\dot{\mathbf{q}}) \\ + \mathbf{C} + \mathbf{G} + \mathbf{M}[\mathbf{I} - \mathbf{M}^{-1}\mathbf{J}^T(\mathbf{J}\mathbf{M}^{-1}\mathbf{J}^T)^{-1}\mathbf{J}]\mathbf{M}^{-1}\mathbf{u}_0. \tag{2.33}$$

The compensation of the forces $\mathbf{C} + \mathbf{G}$ in joint-space is often desirable for this metric in order to have full control over the resolution of the redundancy as gravity compensation purely in task space often results in postures that conflict with joint limits and other parts of the robot.

2.3.2.3 Further Metrics

Using constant parametric matrices as metric, e.g., the identity matrix $\mathbf{N} = \mathbf{I}$, allows us to create alternative, novel approaches. This metric could be of interest as it distributes the "load" created by the task evenly on the actuators. This metric results in a control law

$$\mathbf{u} = (\mathbf{J}\mathbf{M}^{-1})^{+}(\ddot{\mathbf{x}}_d + \mathbf{K}_D(\dot{\mathbf{x}}_d - \dot{\mathbf{x}}) + \mathbf{K}_P(\mathbf{x}_d - \mathbf{x}) - \dot{\mathbf{J}}(\mathbf{q})\dot{\mathbf{q}} \\ + \mathbf{J}\mathbf{M}^{-1}(\mathbf{C} + \mathbf{G})) + (\mathbf{I} - (\mathbf{J}\mathbf{M}^{-1})^{+}\mathbf{J}\mathbf{M}^{-1})\mathbf{u}_1. \tag{2.34}$$

To our knowledge, this controller has not been presented in the literature.

Another practical idea would be to weight the joints depending on the maximal torques $\tau_{\max,i}$ of each joint, e.g., using $\mathbf{N} = \mathrm{diag}(\tau_{\max,1}^{-1}, \ldots, \tau_{\max,n}^{-1})$.

These alternative metrics may be particularly interesting for practical application where the user wants to have more control over the natural appearance of movement, and worry less about the exact theoretical properties – humanoid robotics, for instance, is one of such applications. In some cases, it also may not be possible to have accurate access to complex metrics like the inertia matrix, and simplier metrics will be more suitable.

2.3.3 Controlling Constrained Manipulators: Impedance & Hybrid Control

Contact with outside objects alters the robot's dynamics, i.e., a generalized contact force $\mathbf{F}_C \in \mathbb{R}^6$ acting on the end-effector changes the dynamics of the robot to

$$\mathbf{u} = \mathbf{M}(\mathbf{q})\ddot{\mathbf{q}} + \mathbf{C}(\mathbf{q}, \dot{\mathbf{q}}) + \mathbf{G}(\mathbf{q}) + \mathbf{J}^T\mathbf{F}_C. \tag{2.35}$$

In this case, the interaction between the robot and the environment has to be controlled. This kind of control can both be used to make the interaction with the environment safe (e.g., in a manipulation task) as well as to use the robot to simulate a behavior (e.g., in a haptic display task). We will discuss impedance control and hybrid control as examples of the application of the proposed framework; however, further control ideas such as parallel control can be treated in this framework, too.

2.3.3.1 Impedance Control

In impedance control, we want the robot to simulate the behavior of a mechanical system such as

$$\mathbf{M}_d(\ddot{\mathbf{x}}_d - \ddot{\mathbf{x}}) + \mathbf{D}_d(\dot{\mathbf{x}}_d - \dot{\mathbf{x}}) + \mathbf{P}_d(\mathbf{x}_d - \mathbf{x}) = \mathbf{F}_C, \tag{2.36}$$

where $\mathbf{M}_d \in \mathbb{R}^{6\times 6}$ denotes the mass matrix of a desired simulated dynamical system, $\mathbf{D}_d \in \mathbb{R}^6$ denotes the desired damping, $\mathbf{P}_d \in \mathbb{R}^6$ denotes the gains towards the desired position, and $\mathbf{F}_C \in \mathbb{R}^6$ the forces that result from this particular dynamical behavior. Using Equation (2.27) from Section 2.3.2, we see that this approach can be brought in the standard form for tasks by

$$\mathbf{M}_d\mathbf{J}\ddot{\mathbf{q}} = \mathbf{F}_C - \mathbf{M}_d\ddot{\mathbf{x}}_d - \mathbf{D}_d(\dot{\mathbf{x}}_d - \mathbf{J}\dot{\mathbf{q}}) - \mathbf{P}_d(\mathbf{x}_d - \mathbf{f}(\mathbf{q})) - \mathbf{M}_d\dot{\mathbf{J}}\dot{\mathbf{q}}. \tag{2.37}$$

Thus, we can infer the task description

$$\begin{aligned} \mathbf{A} &= \mathbf{M}_d\mathbf{J}, \\ \mathbf{b} &= \mathbf{F}_C - \mathbf{M}_d\ddot{\mathbf{x}}_d - \mathbf{D}_d(\mathbf{J}\dot{\mathbf{q}} - \dot{\mathbf{x}}_d) - \mathbf{P}_d(\mathbf{f}(\mathbf{q}) - \mathbf{x}_d) - \mathbf{M}_d\dot{\mathbf{J}}\dot{\mathbf{q}}, \end{aligned} \tag{2.38}$$

and apply our framework for deriving the robot control law as shown before.

Kinematic Separation of Simulated System and the Manipulator As in end-effector tracking control, $\mathbf{N} = \mathbf{M}^{-2}$ is a practical metric which basically separates the simulated dynamic system from the physical structure of the manipulator on a kinematic level. For simplicity, we make use of the joint-space control law $\mathbf{u}_1 = \mathbf{C} + \mathbf{G} + \mathbf{u}_0$ similar as before. This results in the control law

$$\begin{aligned} \mathbf{u} &= \mathbf{u}_1 + \mathbf{N}^{-1/2}(\mathbf{A}\mathbf{M}^{-1}\mathbf{N}^{-1/2})^+(\mathbf{b} - \mathbf{A}\mathbf{M}^{-1}(\mathbf{F} + \mathbf{u}_1)), \\ &= \mathbf{M}(\mathbf{M}_d\mathbf{J})^+(\mathbf{F}_C - \mathbf{M}_d\ddot{\mathbf{x}}_d - \mathbf{D}_d(\mathbf{J}\dot{\mathbf{q}} - \dot{\mathbf{x}}_d) - \mathbf{P}_d(\mathbf{f}(\mathbf{q}) - \mathbf{x}_d) - \mathbf{M}_d\dot{\mathbf{J}}\dot{\mathbf{q}}) \\ &\quad + \mathbf{C} + \mathbf{G} + (\mathbf{I} - \mathbf{M}(\mathbf{M}_d\mathbf{J})^+\mathbf{M}_d\mathbf{J}\mathbf{M}^{-1})\mathbf{u}_0. \end{aligned} \tag{2.39}$$

As $(\mathbf{M}_d\mathbf{J})^+ = \mathbf{J}^T\mathbf{M}_d(\mathbf{M}_d\mathbf{J}\mathbf{J}^T\mathbf{M}_d)^{-1} = \mathbf{J}^+\mathbf{M}_d^{-1}$ since $\mathbf{M}_d$ is invertible, we can simplify this control law to become

$$\begin{aligned} \mathbf{u} &= \mathbf{M}\mathbf{J}^+\mathbf{M}_d^{-1}(\mathbf{F}_C - \mathbf{M}_d\ddot{\mathbf{x}}_d - \mathbf{D}_d(\mathbf{J}\dot{\mathbf{q}} - \dot{\mathbf{x}}_d) - \mathbf{P}_d(\mathbf{f}(\mathbf{q}) - \mathbf{x}_d)) \\ &\quad - \mathbf{M}\mathbf{J}^+\dot{\mathbf{J}}\dot{\mathbf{q}} + \mathbf{C} + \mathbf{G} + \mathbf{M}(\mathbf{I} - \mathbf{J}^+\mathbf{J})\mathbf{M}^{-1}\mathbf{u}_0. \end{aligned} \tag{2.40}$$

We note that $\ddot{\mathbf{x}}_d = \mathbf{M}_d^{-1}(\mathbf{F}_C - \mathbf{M}_d\ddot{\mathbf{x}}_d - \mathbf{D}_d(\mathbf{J}\dot{\mathbf{q}} - \dot{\mathbf{x}}_d) - \mathbf{P}_d(\mathbf{f}(\mathbf{q}) - \mathbf{x}_d))$ is a desired acceleration in task-space. This insight clarifies the previous remark about the separation of the simulated system and the actual physical system: we have one system which describes the interaction with the environment – and additionally we use a second, inverse-model type controller to execute the desired accelerations with our robot arm.

Dynamically Consistent Combination As in end-effector control $\mathbf{N} = \mathbf{M}^{-1}$ is a practical metric which combines both the simulated and the physical dynamic systems employing Gauss' principle. For simplicity, we make use of the joint-space control law $\mathbf{u}_1 = \mathbf{C} + \mathbf{G} + \mathbf{u}_0$ as before. This approach results in the control law

$$\begin{aligned}\mathbf{u} &= \mathbf{u}_1 + \mathbf{N}^{-1/2}(\mathbf{A}\mathbf{M}^{-1}\mathbf{N}^{-1/2})^{+}(\mathbf{b} - \mathbf{A}\mathbf{M}^{-1}(\mathbf{F} + \mathbf{u}_1)),\\ &= \mathbf{u}_1 + \mathbf{J}^T(\mathbf{J}\mathbf{M}^{-1}\mathbf{J}^T)^{-1}(\mathbf{b} - \mathbf{A}\mathbf{M}^{-1}(\mathbf{F} + \mathbf{u}_1)),\\ &= \mathbf{M}^{1/2}(\mathbf{M}_d\mathbf{J}\mathbf{M}^{-1/2})^{+}(\mathbf{F}_C - \mathbf{D}_d(\mathbf{J}\dot{\mathbf{q}} - \dot{\mathbf{x}}_d) - \mathbf{P}_d(\mathbf{f}(\mathbf{q}) - \mathbf{x}_d) - \mathbf{M}_d\dot{\mathbf{J}}\dot{\mathbf{q}})\\ &+ \mathbf{C} + \mathbf{G} + (\mathbf{I} - \mathbf{M}(\mathbf{M}_d\mathbf{J})^{+}\mathbf{M}_d\mathbf{J}\mathbf{M}^{-1})\mathbf{u}_0. \end{aligned} \tag{2.41}$$

As $(\mathbf{M}_d\mathbf{J}\mathbf{M}^{-1/2})^{+} = \mathbf{M}^{-1/2}\mathbf{J}^T(\mathbf{J}\mathbf{M}^{-1}\mathbf{J}^T)^{-1}\mathbf{M}_d^{-1}$ since $\mathbf{M}_d$ is invertible, we can simplify this control law into

$$\begin{aligned}\mathbf{u} &= \mathbf{J}^T(\mathbf{J}\mathbf{M}^{-1}\mathbf{J}^T)^{-1}\mathbf{M}_d^{-1}(\mathbf{F}_C - \mathbf{D}_d(\mathbf{J}\dot{\mathbf{q}} - \dot{\mathbf{x}}_d) - \mathbf{P}_d(\mathbf{f}(\mathbf{q}) - \mathbf{x}_d))\\ &- \mathbf{M}\mathbf{J}^{+}\dot{\mathbf{J}}\dot{\mathbf{q}} + \mathbf{C} + \mathbf{G} + (\mathbf{I} - \mathbf{M}\mathbf{J}^{+}\mathbf{J}\mathbf{M}^{-1})\mathbf{u}_0. \end{aligned} \tag{2.42}$$

We note that the main difference between this and the previous impedance control law is the location of the matrix $\mathbf{M}$.

2.3.3.2 Hybrid Control

In hybrid control, we intend to control the desired position of the end-effector $\mathbf{x}_d$ and the desired contact force exerted by the end-effector $\mathbf{F}_d$. Modern hybrid control approaches are essentially similar to our introduced framework (De Wit et al., 1996). Both are inspired by constrained motion and use this insight in order to achieve the desired task. In traditional hybrid control, a natural or artificial, idealized holomonic constraint $\phi(\mathbf{q}, t) = 0$ acts on our manipulator, and subsequently the direction of the forces is determined through the virtual work principle of d'Alembert. We can make significant contributions here as our framework is a generalization of Gauss' principle that allows us to handle even non-holomic constraints $\phi(\mathbf{q}, \dot{\mathbf{q}}, t) = 0$ as long as they are given in the form

$$\mathbf{A}_\phi(\mathbf{q}, \dot{\mathbf{q}})\ddot{\mathbf{q}} = \mathbf{b}_\phi(\mathbf{q}, \dot{\mathbf{q}}). \tag{2.43}$$

$\mathbf{A}_\phi$, $\mathbf{b}_\phi$ depend on the type of the constraint, e.g., for time-invariant, holomonic constraints $\phi(\mathbf{q}) = 0$, we would have $\mathbf{A}_\phi(\mathbf{q}, \dot{\mathbf{q}}) = \mathbf{J}_\phi$ and $\mathbf{b}_\phi(\mathbf{q}, \dot{\mathbf{q}}) = -\dot{\mathbf{J}}_\phi\dot{\mathbf{q}}$ with $\mathbf{J}_\phi = \partial\phi/\partial\mathbf{q}$ as in (De Wit et al., 1996). Additionally, we intend to exert the contact force $\mathbf{F}_d$ in the task; this can be achieved if we choose the joint-space control law

$$\mathbf{u}_1 = \mathbf{C} + \mathbf{G} + \mathbf{J}_\phi^T\mathbf{F}_d. \tag{2.44}$$

From the previous discussion, this constraint is achieved by the control law

$$\mathbf{u} = \mathbf{u}_1 + \mathbf{N}^{-1/2}(\mathbf{A}_\phi\mathbf{M}^{-1}\mathbf{N}^{-1/2})^+(\mathbf{b}_\phi - \mathbf{A}_\phi\mathbf{M}^{-1}(\mathbf{F}+\mathbf{u}_1)), \tag{2.45}$$

$$= \mathbf{C}+\mathbf{G}+\mathbf{N}^{-1/2}(\mathbf{A}_\phi\mathbf{M}^{-1}\mathbf{N}^{-1/2})^+\mathbf{b}_\phi \tag{2.46}$$

$$+\mathbf{N}^{-1/2}(\mathbf{I}-(\mathbf{A}\mathbf{M}^{-1}\mathbf{N}^{-1/2})^+\mathbf{A}\mathbf{M}^{-1}\mathbf{N}^{-1/2})\mathbf{N}^{1/2}\mathbf{J}_\phi^T\mathbf{F}_d.$$

Note that the exerted forces act in the null-space of the achieved tracking task; therefore both the constraint and the force can be set independently.

2.4 Evaluations

The main contribution of this book chapter is the unifying methodology for deriving robot controllers. Each of the presented controllers is a well founded control law which, from a theoretical point of view, would not need require empirical evaluations, particularly as most of the control laws are already well-known from the literature and their stability properties have been explored before. Nevertheless, it is useful to highlight one component in the suggested framework, i.e., the impact of the metric $\mathbf{N}$ on the particular performance of a controller. For this purpose, we chose to evaluate the three end-effector controllers from Section 2.3.2: (i) the resolved-acceleration kinematic controller (with metric $\mathbf{N} = \mathbf{M}^{-2}$) in Equation (2.32), (ii) Khatib's operational space control law ($\mathbf{N} = \mathbf{M}^{-1}$) in Equation (2.33), and (iii) the identity metric control law ($\mathbf{N} = \mathbf{I}$) in Equation (2.34).

As an experimental platform, we used the Sarcos Dextrous Master Arm, a hydraulic manipulator with an anthropomorphic design shown in Figure 2.2 (b). Its seven degrees of freedom mimic the major degrees of freedom of the human arm, i.e., there are three DOFs in the shoulder, one in the elbow and three in the wrist. The robot's end-effector was supposed to track a planar "figure-eight (8)" pattern in task space at two different speeds. In order to stabilize the null-space trajectories, we choose a PD control law in joint space which pulls the robot towards a fixed rest posture, $\mathbf{q}_{\text{rest}}$, given by

$$\mathbf{u}_0 = \mathbf{M}(\mathbf{K}_{P_0}(\mathbf{q}_{\text{rest}} - \mathbf{q}) - \mathbf{K}_{D_0}\dot{\mathbf{q}}). \tag{2.47}$$

Additionally we apply gravity, centrifugal and Coriolis force compensation, such that $\mathbf{u}_1 = \mathbf{u}_0 + \mathbf{C} + \mathbf{G}$. For consistency, all three controllers are assigned the same gains both for the task and joint space stabilization.

Figure 2.3 shows the end-point trajectories of the three controllers in a slow pattern of eight seconds per cycle "figure-eight (8)". Figure 2.4 shows a faster pace of four seconds per cycle. All three controllers have similar end-point trajectories and result in fairly accurate task achievement. Each one has an offset from the desired trajectory (thin black line), primarily due to the imperfect dynamics model of the robot. The root mean squared errors (RMS) between the actual and the desired trajectory in task-space for each of the controllers are shown in the Table 2.1.

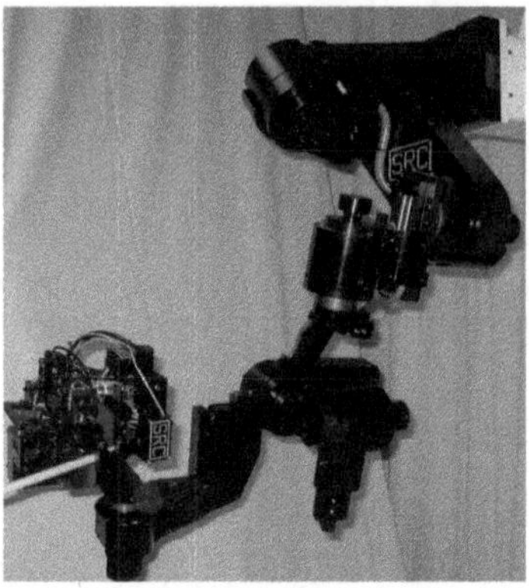

Figure 2.2: Sarcos Master Arm robot, as used for the evaluations on our experiments.

While the performance of the three controllers is very similar in task space, we did notice that the resolved-acceleration kinematic controller ($\mathbf{N} = \mathbf{M}^{-2}$) had a slight advantage. The reason for this performance difference is most likely due to errors in the dynamics model which affect the three control laws differently, i.e., the effect of these errors is amplified by the inversion of the mass matrix in the control laws given in Equations (2.33, 2.34) while the decoupling of the dynamics and kinematics provided by the controller in Equation (2.32) can be favorable as the effect of modeling errors is not increased. More accurate model parameters of the manipulator's rigid body dynamics would result in a reduction of the difference between these control laws (observable in Figures 2.3 and 2.4) as we have confirmed in simulations.

Figure 2.5 illustrates how the joint space trajectories appear for the fast cycle. Although end-point trajectories were very similar, joint space trajectories differ significantly due to the different optimization criteria of each control law, which emphasizes the importance of the choice of the metric $\mathbf{N}$.

Table 2.1: This table shows the root mean squared error results of the tracking achieved by the different control laws.

Metric	Slow RMS error [m]	Fast RMS error [m]
$\mathbf{N} = \mathbf{M}^{-2}$	0.0122	0.0130
$\mathbf{N} = \mathbf{M}^{-1}$	0.0126	0.0136
$\mathbf{N} = \mathbf{I}$	0.0130	0.0140

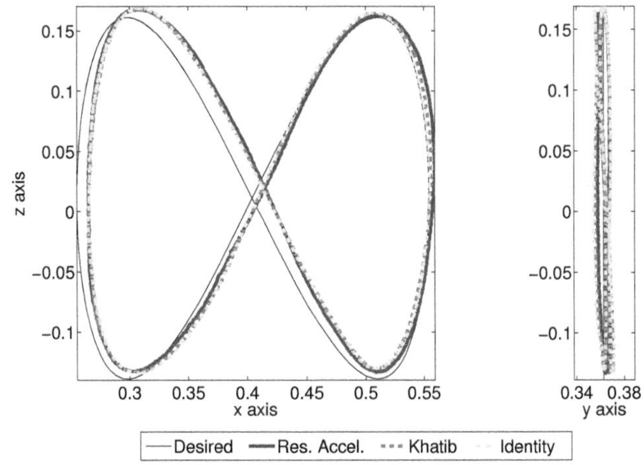

Figure 2.3: This figure shows the three end-effector trajectory controllers tracking a "figure eight (8)" pattern at 8 seconds per cycle. On the left is the x-z plane with the y-z plane on the right. All units are in meters.

2.5 Conclusion & Discussion

In order to conclude this book chapter, we give an overview on the contributions of the chapter and outline the most important open problems for future research.

2.5.1 Contributions of the Chapter

In this book chapter, we have presented an optimal control framework which allows the development of a unified approach for deriving a number of different robot control laws for rigid body dynamics systems. We demonstrated how we can make use of both the robot model and a task description in order to create control laws which are optimal with respect to the squared motor command under a particular metric while *perfectly* fulfilling the task *at each instant of time*. We have discussed how to realize stability both in task as well as in joint-space for this framework.

Building on this foundation, we demonstrated how a variety of control laws–which on first inspection appear rather unrelated to one another–can be derived using this straightforward framework. The covered types of tasks include joint-space trajectory control for both fully actuated and overactuated robots, end-effector trajectory control, impedance and hybrid control.

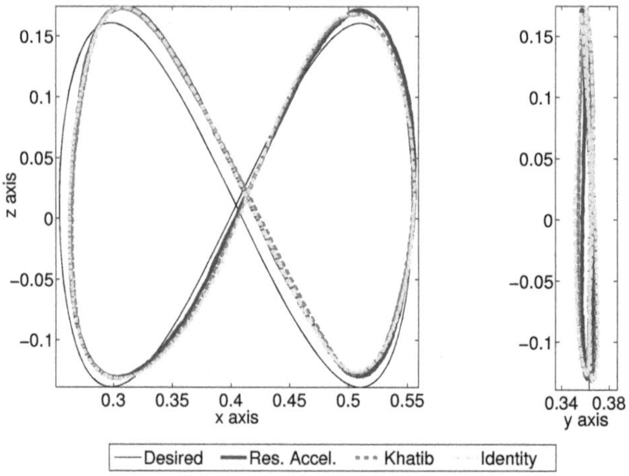

Figure 2.4: The same three controllers tracking the same "figure eight (8)" pattern at a faster pace of 4 seconds per cycle. The labels and units remain the same as in Figure 2.3.

The implemention of three of the end-effector trajectory control laws resulting from our unified framework on a real-world Sarcos Master Arm robot was carried out as an empirical evaluation. As expected, the behavior in task space is very similar for all three control laws; yet, they result in very different joint-space behaviors due to the different cost functions resulting from the different metrics of each control law.

The major contribution of this book chapter is the unified framework that we have developed. It allows a derivation of a variety of previously known controllers, and promises easy development of a host of novel ones, in particular control laws with additional constraints. The particular controllers reported in this book chapter were selected primarly for illustarting the applicability of this framework and demonstrating its strength in unifying different control algorithms using a common building principle.

The work presented in this chapter up to this point has been presented in (Peters et al., 2005; Peters, Mistry, Udwadia, & Schaal, 2005) and the resulting journal paper is currently under review at Autonomous Robots.

2.5.2 Extension to Infinite Horizon Optimality

It is quite obvious that the point-wise minimization of the instantanious motor commands $\mathbf{u}^T\mathbf{u}$ does not neccessarily result in a minimization of $\int_0^\infty \mathbf{u}^T\mathbf{u}dt$ if there is more than

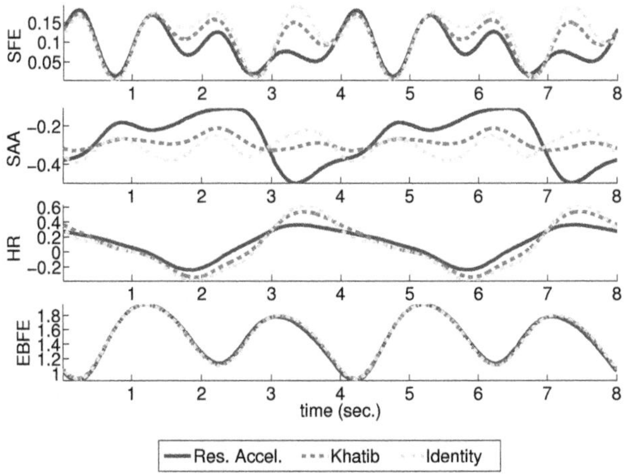

Figure 2.5: Joint space trajectories for the four major degrees of freedom, i.e., shoulder flexion-extension (SFE), shoulder adduction-abduction (SAA), humeral rotation (HR) and elbow flexion-extension (EBFE), are shown here. Joint angle units are in radians. The labels are identical to the ones in Figure 2.3.

one solution $\mathbf{u}$ fulfilling the task $\mathbf{A}\ddot{\mathbf{q}} = \mathbf{b}$. For example, assume that there are two paths in joint-space at a point in time which both fulfill $\mathbf{A}\ddot{\mathbf{q}} = \mathbf{b}$ and you have to choose between the two of them. In this case, we could end up choosing a path which requires the lower immediate torque at that instant of time but much higher torque for the rest of the trajectory, resulting into a higher average torque. Unfortunately, such tasks exist frequently for redundant robots and, thus, it is of high importance to understand what the infinite horizon implications of this method are. Following the work by Kazerounian & Wang (1988), we can compute the infinite horizon optimal controller for a different measure, i.e., the amount of kinetic energy of a holonomic task[3] plus the value of the storage function (which allows additional position-based punishments).

Proposition 2.5 *The minimization of*

$$J_\infty = \int_0^\infty \left[\dot{\mathbf{q}}^T \mathbf{N}_\infty (\mathbf{q}, t) \dot{\mathbf{q}} + V(\mathbf{q})\right] dt \tag{2.48}$$

[3]The same metric is commonly used as a base in differential geometric methods (Bullo & Lewis, 2004).

subjected to a holonomic task $\mathbf{h}(\mathbf{q},t)=0$ *in form of* $\mathbf{A}\ddot{\mathbf{q}}=\mathbf{b}$ *and a mechanical system* $\mathbf{u}=\mathbf{M}\ddot{\mathbf{q}}+\mathbf{F}$*, yields the control law*

$$\mathbf{u}=\mathbf{u}_0(\mathbf{q})+\mathbf{M}(\mathbf{A}\mathbf{N}_\infty^{-1/2})^+\left[\mathbf{b}+\mathbf{A}\mathbf{N}_\infty(\mathbf{u}_0(\mathbf{q})-\mathbf{F})\right], \tag{2.49}$$

with a joint-space control law

$$\mathbf{u}_0(\mathbf{q})=\dot{\mathbf{N}}_\infty\dot{\mathbf{q}}-\mathbf{B}\dot{\mathbf{q}}-V'(\mathbf{q})+\mathbf{F} \tag{2.50}$$

where $\mathbf{B}=\partial\left(\dot{\mathbf{q}}^T\mathbf{N}_\infty\right)/\partial\mathbf{q}$*.*

Proof. Using an instantaneous cost function

$$c(\mathbf{q},\dot{\mathbf{q}},t)=\dot{\mathbf{q}}^T\mathbf{N}_\infty^{-1}(\mathbf{q},t)\,\dot{\mathbf{q}}+V(\mathbf{q})+\boldsymbol{\mu}^T\mathbf{h}(q,t). \tag{2.51}$$

The resulting Euler equations $(\partial c/\partial\mathbf{q})-d(\partial c/\partial\dot{\mathbf{q}})/dt=\mathbf{0}$ can be reformulated as

$$2\mathbf{N}_\infty\ddot{\mathbf{q}}+V'(\mathbf{q})+2\dot{\mathbf{N}}_\infty\dot{\mathbf{q}}-\mathbf{B}\dot{\mathbf{q}}-\mathbf{A}^T\boldsymbol{\mu}=\mathbf{0}, \tag{2.52}$$

where $\mathbf{B}=\partial\left(\dot{\mathbf{q}}^T\mathbf{N}_\infty\right)/\partial\mathbf{q}$. This equations yields the acceleration

$$\ddot{\mathbf{q}}=0.5\mathbf{N}_\infty^{-1}\left(\mathbf{B}\dot{\mathbf{q}}+\mathbf{A}^T\boldsymbol{\mu}-2\dot{\mathbf{N}}_\infty\dot{\mathbf{q}}-V'(\mathbf{q})\right). \tag{2.53}$$

Substituting into $\mathbf{A}\ddot{\mathbf{q}}=\mathbf{b}$ yields $\boldsymbol{\mu}$, resubstituting in Equation (2.53) and using $\mathbf{u}=\mathbf{M}\ddot{\mathbf{q}}+\mathbf{F}$, we obtain Equation (2.49). ■

Note that this approach is significantly more limited. It requires the constraints to be holonomic in nature, the null-space control law cannot include differential terms and will be drastically more difficult to compute. However, from this infinite horizon optimal controller, we can infer an important statement on the infinite horizon optimality of some control laws.

Proposition 2.6 *The point-wise optimal controller with cost function*

$$J_0=(\mathbf{u}-\mathbf{u}_0)^T\mathbf{N}_0(\mathbf{q},t)(\mathbf{u}-\mathbf{u}_0) \tag{2.54}$$

is equivalent to the one minimizing the infinite horizon cost in Equation (2.48) for $\mathbf{N}_0(\mathbf{q},t)=\mathbf{M}^{-1}(\mathbf{q})\,\mathbf{N}_\infty(\mathbf{q},t)\,\mathbf{M}^{-1}(\mathbf{q})$ *and a joint-space control law*

$$\mathbf{u}_0(\mathbf{q})=\dot{\mathbf{N}}_\infty\dot{\mathbf{q}}-\mathbf{B}\dot{\mathbf{q}}-V'(\mathbf{q})+\mathbf{F} \tag{2.55}$$

where $\mathbf{B}=\partial\left(\dot{\mathbf{q}}^T\mathbf{N}_\infty\right)/\partial\mathbf{q}$*.*

Proof. We compare the optimal control laws from Equations (2.49) and (2.6). The result directly follows. ■

For $\mathbf{N}_0(\mathbf{q},t) = \mathbf{M}^{-1}(\mathbf{q})$ and $\mathbf{G}(\mathbf{q}) = V'(\mathbf{q})$, this implies that no special joint-space control law is needed for infinite-horizon optimality. This artifact is a result of the special nature of $\mathbf{M}(\mathbf{q})$ being the metric found in mechanics and has been established in a different setting by Doty et al. (1993) and Udwadia (Udwadia & Kalaba, 1996). For $\mathbf{N}_0(\mathbf{q},t) = \mathbf{M}^{-2}(\mathbf{q})$, and small $\dot{\mathbf{q}}$, we can ensure $\mathbf{G}(\mathbf{q}) + \mathbf{C}(\mathbf{q},\dot{\mathbf{q}}) \approx V'(\mathbf{q})$ and thus have a similar equivalence. This explains why these metrics have been preferred in the theory of robot control. Nevertheless, there are strong arguments against using these metrics as the required motor commands can be infinite for intertia matrix related metrics, see (Udwadia & Kalaba, 1996).

The infinite horizon point of view allows us to make two very strong points, i.e., that adding a null-space control law which includes velocities alters the infinite-horizon metric for which the controller is optimal, and that the hierachical extension cannot be optimal from infinite horizon point of view.

2.5.2.1 Extension of the Infinite Horizon Optimality using Storage Functions

If we intend to have joint-space control laws as the ones suggested in this paper, e.g., a spring-damper system in joint-space (or even complex ones), then we need to replace $V(\mathbf{q})$ by $V(\mathbf{q},\dot{\mathbf{q}})$, e.g., $V(\mathbf{q},\dot{\mathbf{q}}) = K_D\dot{\mathbf{q}}^2 + K_P(\mathbf{q}_d - \mathbf{q})^2$ for a spring-damper system in joint-space. This will alter the metric of the system significantly.

Proposition 2.7 *For velocity dependent $V(\mathbf{q},\dot{\mathbf{q}})$, the infinite horizon optimal control law corresponds to the point-wise optimal control law with the altered metric*

$$\mathbf{N}_0 = \mathbf{M}^{-1}(\mathbf{q}) \left[\mathbf{N}_\infty(\mathbf{q},t) + \frac{\partial^2 V}{\partial \dot{\mathbf{q}}^2}\right] \mathbf{M}^{-1}(\mathbf{q}), \tag{2.56}$$

with a joint-space control law

$$\mathbf{u}_0(\mathbf{q}) = \dot{\mathbf{N}}_\infty \dot{\mathbf{q}} - \mathbf{B}\dot{\mathbf{q}} - \frac{\partial V}{\partial \mathbf{q}} + \frac{\partial^2 V}{\partial \dot{\mathbf{q}} \partial \mathbf{q}} \dot{\mathbf{q}} + \mathbf{F}. \tag{2.57}$$

Proof. We replace $V(\mathbf{q})$ by $V(\mathbf{q},\dot{\mathbf{q}})$ in Proposition 2.5, which implies that $V'(\mathbf{q})$ needs to be replaced by $\partial V/\partial\mathbf{q} - (\partial^2 V/\partial\dot{\mathbf{q}}^2)\ddot{\mathbf{q}} - (\partial^2 V/\partial\dot{\mathbf{q}}\partial\mathbf{q})\dot{\mathbf{q}}$. When following the steps of Proposition 2.5 from here on, the step follows naturally. ■

This point puts a strong doubt on the idea that an inertia metric is always that useful: the main advantage of the inertia metric is that it directly results in an energy optimal joint-space control law. However, a necessary condition for joint-space stability is that the joint-space control laws has a velocity component as shown in Example 2.1. Thus, this alteration of the metric will be necessary in all practical cases.

2.5.2.2 Re-evaluation of the Hierachical Extension

The hierachical extension opens up a variety of important questions not tackled in the literature. Already on the two level hierchachy (i.e., a joint-space control law and a task space control law), the joint-space control law can best be interpreted as an additional storage function and will always act as a form of friction, thus increasing the amount of energy consumed by the system. Obviously, a n-level hiercharchy has no physical interpretation for $n > 2$ and, to date, there is no way of showing an infinite horizon optimal control law. Even worse, when re-evaluating the derivations in Proposition (2.5) for hierachical approaches, it is straightforward to show that a hierachical approach cannot be developed in a similar fashion. Instead, a hierachical control law which is optimal from an infinite horizon point of view, will require higher-order derivatives such as $\dddot{\mathbf{q}}$ for $n = 3$, $\dddot{\mathbf{q}}$ and $\ddddot{\mathbf{q}}$ for $n = 4$, and $\dddot{\mathbf{q}}, \ldots, \mathbf{q}^{(n)}$ for arbitrary n. The requirement of these higher order derivatives for infinite horizon optimality might be cause serious trouble for the hierachical approach.

Furthermore, the hierachical extension might not even be desirable as all tasks with exception of the top-level task can be degraded arbitrarily in tracking performance in the hierachical approach. Thus, it might be smarter to consider a weighted approach where the tasks are combined in a form

$$\mathbf{A} = [w_1\mathbf{A}_1, w_2\mathbf{A}_2, \ldots, w_n\mathbf{A}_n], \quad (2.58)$$

$$\mathbf{b} = [w_1\mathbf{b}_1, w_2\mathbf{b}_2, \ldots, w_n\mathbf{b}_n], \quad (2.59)$$

where w_i denotes the weight of the task i. In such approaches, a larger $w_i \gg w_j$ will ensure that in the overconstrained case, task j is largely overruled by task i. However, it will happen in a soft and not in a hard way; thus, if both can be fulfilled, they will be fulfilled without contradiction. For the hierachical approach discussed, task fulfillment cannot always be guaranteed for lower level tasks even if it is possible as the higher level task can simply overrule the lower level task even if an alternative which fulfills both higher and lower task is possible.

2.5.3 Future Work

Among the other interesting prospective topics resulting from this chapter are the application to more complex tasks and systems and using this method for planning.

2.5.3.1 Complex Systems

In this book chapter, we have only evaluated the more general systems and intend to point out the most important systems which should be evaluated with this approach in the future. One important topic is the control of systems are *overactuated systems* which have more actuaters than degrees of freedom, i.e., redundancy on the torque generation level as it exists in biological systems where hundreds of muscles interact. While we have suggested a basic solution to this problem (Peters et al., 2005), a proper evaluation of overactuated control based upon the approach suggested in this paper could result in interesting insights both for biological motor control as well as robotics.

Controlling *underactuated systems* is probably the most important robot control problem as they occur frequently in nature, e.g., legged locomotion, and even simple toy systems such as cart-pole balancing fall into this category. From the viewpoint of the approach descriped in this chapter, an underactuated control problem can be treated as a modified task where we have

$$\begin{bmatrix} \mathbf{A} \\ \mathbf{m}_1^T \\ \vdots \\ \mathbf{m}_k^T \end{bmatrix} \ddot{\mathbf{q}} = \begin{bmatrix} \mathbf{b} \\ F_1 \\ \vdots \\ F_k \end{bmatrix} \tag{2.60}$$

with the actual control task $\mathbf{A}\ddot{\mathbf{q}} = \mathbf{b}$, and, the additional constraint for the unactuated degrees of freedom $i \in \{1, \ldots, k\}$, we always have $u_i = 0$ or $\mathbf{m}_i^T \ddot{\mathbf{q}} = F_i$. Here, $\mathbf{m}_i^T$ denotes the i-th row of the inertia matrix. It becomes clear from this formulation, that underactuated systems can be treated in the same way as a fully actuated one as long as the task can be fulfilled. If the task cannot be fulfilled, i.e., if the problem is overconstrained, this becomes a pure planning problem where only the task planner can ensure that **any** control law can ever perform the task. The same holds true for *non-holonomic systems*, where the non-holonomic constraints can result in an overconstrained control task with the same difficulties as for underactuated systems.

2.5.3.2 Applications in Planning

One important aspect might arise out of the application of this method to overactuated systems, i.e., one might be able to realize a *dimensionality reduction* method which allows planning of controllable trajectories in a lower-dimensional domain. While this idea is similar to the goal of differential geometric control methods, it might arise naturally from decompositions of the matrix $(AMN^{-1/2})^+$. Such approaches could be similar to the one suggested in Section 8.4.1 in (Udwadia & Kalaba, 1996) and, the same time, would become the foundations of novel machine learning algorithms.

Similarly, the methods proposed in this chapter have another interesting implication for planning of tasks as they can be used for feasibility tests of trajectories in simulation. The resulting mechanism is quite simple: if the planned trajectory (or task) is controllable at all, the control law generated by this method will be able to control it in an idealized simulation. Thus, plans can be evaluated for their feasibility. While this might appear trivial, it can be very useful in practice.

Chapter 3

Learning Tracking Control in Operational Space

An approximate solution to the right problem is far better than an exact answer to an approximate problem.
John Wilder Tukey (American statistician, 1915-2000)

One of the control problems which we have discussed in Chapter 2 is tracking control in operational space. While operational space control is of essential importance for robotics and well-understood from an analytical point of view, it can be prohibitively hard to achieve accurate control in face of modeling errors, which are inevitable in complex robots, e.g., humanoid robots. In such cases, learning control methods can offer an interesting alternative to analytical control algorithms. However, the resulting learning problem is ill-defined as it requires to learn an inverse mapping of a usually redundant system, which is well known to suffer from the property of non-convexity of the solution space, i.e., the learning system could generate motor commands that try to steer the robot into physically impossible configurations. A first important insight for this book chapter is that, nevertheless, a physically correct solution to the inverse problem does exit when learning of the inverse map is performed in a suitable piecewise linear way. The second crucial component for our work is based on an insight in Section 2.3.2 that many operational space controllers can be understood in terms of a constrained optimal control problem. The cost function associated with this optimal control problem allows us to formulate a learning algorithm that automatically synthesizes a globally consistent desired resolution of redundancy while learning the operational space controller. From the view of machine learning, the learning problem corresponds to a reinforcement learning problem that maximizes an immediate reward and that employs an expectation-maximization policy search algorithm. Evaluations on a three degrees of freedom robot arm are used illustrate the suggested approach and the application to a physically realistic simulator of the anthropomorphic SARCOS Master arm demonstrates feasibility for complex high degree-of-freedom robots.

3.1 Introduction

Operational space control is one of the most elegant approaches to task control due to its potential for dynamically consistent control, compliant control, force control, hierarchical control, and many other favorable properties, with applications from end-effector control of manipulators (Khatib, 1987; Hsu et al., 1989) up to balancing and gait execution for humanoid robots (Sentis & Khatib, 2005). If the robot model is accurately known, operational space control is well-understood yielding a variety of different solution alternatives, including resolved-motion rate control, resolved-acceleration control, and force-based control (Nakanishi et al., 2005). However, particularly if compliant (i.e., low-gain) control is desired, as in many new robotic systems that are supposed to operate safely in human environments, operational space control becomes increasingly difficult in the presence of unmodeled nonlinearities, leading to reduced accuracy or even unpredictable and unstable null-space behavior in the robot system. As a potential solution to this problem, learning control methods seem to be promising. But learning methods do not easily provide the highly structured knowledge required in traditional operational space control laws, i.e., Jacobians, inertia matrices, and Coriolis/centripetal and gravity forces, as all these terms are not always instantly observable and are therefore not suitable for formulating supervised learning as traditionally used in learning control approaches (Nakanishi, Farrell, & Schaal, 2004).

In this book chapter, we will suggest a novel approach to learning operational space control that avoids extracting such structured knowledge, and rather aims at learning the operational space control law directly. To develop our approach, we will proceed as follows: firstly, we will review operational space control and discuss where learning can be beneficial. Secondly, we will pose operational space control as a learning problem and discuss why standard learning techniques cannot be applied straightforwardly. Using the alternative understanding of operational space control as an optimal control technique, we reformulate it as an immediate reward reinforcement learning or policy search problem and suggest novel algorithms for learning some of the most standard types of operational space control laws. These new techniques are evaluated on a simulated three degree-of-freedom robot arm and a simulated anthropomorphic seven degrees of freedom SARCOS robot arm.

3.1.1 Notation and Remarks

Throughout this book chapter, we assume the standard rigid body model for the description of the robot, i.e.,

$$\mathbf{M}(\mathbf{q})\ddot{\mathbf{q}} + \mathbf{C}(\mathbf{q}, \dot{\mathbf{q}}) + \mathbf{G}(\mathbf{q}) + \boldsymbol{\varepsilon}(\mathbf{q}, \dot{\mathbf{q}}) = \mathbf{u}, \tag{3.1}$$

where $\mathbf{q}$, $\dot{\mathbf{q}}$, $\ddot{\mathbf{q}} \in \mathbb{R}^n$ denote the joint coordinates, velocities and accelerations of the robot, respectively. The torques generated by the motors of the robot, also referred to as motor commands, are given by $\mathbf{u} \in \mathbb{R}^n$. Furthermore, $\mathbf{M}(\mathbf{q})$ denotes the inertia tensor or mass matrix, $\mathbf{C}(\mathbf{q},\dot{\mathbf{q}})$ the Coriolis and centripetal forces, $\mathbf{G}(\mathbf{q})$ is gravity and $\varepsilon(\mathbf{q},\dot{\mathbf{q}})$ denotes unmodeled nonlinearities.

In operational space control, we intend to execute trajectories or forces[1] given in the coordinate system of the actual task. A well-studied example is a robot arm where position and orientation of the end-effector are controlled (Khatib, 1987; Hsu et al., 1989); however, a variety of further applications exist, such as the control of the center of gravity for balancing legged robots, which can also be thought of as operational space control (Sentis & Khatib, 2005). Position and orientation $\mathbf{x}\in\mathbb{R}^m$ of the controlled element of the robot in task-space, e.g., the end-effector, is given by the forward kinematics $\mathbf{x}=\mathbf{f}_{\text{Kinematics}}(\mathbf{q})$. The derivatives yield both velocity and acceleration in task space, i.e.,

$$\dot{\mathbf{x}}=\mathbf{J}(\mathbf{q})\,\dot{\mathbf{q}},\;\ddot{\mathbf{x}}=\mathbf{J}(\mathbf{q})\,\ddot{\mathbf{q}}+\dot{\mathbf{J}}(\mathbf{q})\,\dot{\mathbf{q}}, \tag{3.2}$$

where $\mathbf{J}(\mathbf{q}) = d\mathbf{f}_{\text{Kinematics}}(\mathbf{q})/d\mathbf{q}$ denotes the Jacobian. We assume that the robot is in general redundant, i.e., it has more degrees of freedom than required for the task or, equivalently, $n>m$.

3.1.2 Operational Space Control as an Optimal Control Problem

Using the framework of trajectory tracking as an example, the general problem in operational space control[1] can be described as follows: generate a control law in the form $\mathbf{u}=\mathbf{f}_{\text{Control}}(\mathbf{q},\dot{\mathbf{q}},\mathbf{x}_d,\dot{\mathbf{x}}_d,\ddot{\mathbf{x}}_d)$ which controls the robot along a joint space trajectory $\mathbf{q}(t)$, $\dot{\mathbf{q}}(t)$, and $\ddot{\mathbf{q}}(t)$,such that the controlled element (e.g., the end-effector) follows a desired trajectory in task space $\mathbf{x}_d(t)$, $\dot{\mathbf{x}}_d(t)$, and $\ddot{\mathbf{x}}_d(t)$. This problem has been thoroughly discussed since the late 1980s (e.g., (Khatib, 1987; Hsu et al., 1989)) and, among others, has resulted in a class of well-known control laws (Nakanishi et al., 2005). As an important new insight into operational space control it was recently discovered (Peters et al., 2005), that many of the suggested controllers in the literature can be derived as the solution of a constrained optimization problem given by

$$\min_{\mathbf{u}} C_0(\mathbf{u})=\mathbf{u}^T\mathbf{N}\mathbf{u}\text{ s.t. }\mathbf{J}\ddot{\mathbf{q}}=\ddot{\mathbf{x}}_{\text{ref}}-\dot{\mathbf{J}}\dot{\mathbf{q}}, \tag{3.3}$$

where $\mathbf{N}$ denotes a positive definite metric that weights the contribution of the motor commands to the cost function, and $\ddot{\mathbf{x}}_{\text{ref}}=\ddot{\mathbf{x}}_d(t)+\mathbf{K}_d(\dot{\mathbf{x}}_d(t)-\dot{\mathbf{x}}(t))+\mathbf{K}_p(\mathbf{x}_d(t)-\mathbf{x}(t))$ denotes a reference attractor in task space with gain matrices $\mathbf{K}_d$ and $\mathbf{K}_p$. The resulting control laws or solution of this optimization problem obey the general form (Peters et al., 2005)

$$\mathbf{u}=\mathbf{N}^{-1/2}(\mathbf{J}\mathbf{M}^{-1}\mathbf{N}^{-1/2})^{+}(\ddot{\mathbf{x}}_{\text{ref}}-\dot{\mathbf{J}}\dot{\mathbf{q}}+\mathbf{J}\mathbf{M}^{-1}\mathbf{F}), \tag{3.4}$$

[1] In the more general case, the hybrid creation of forces in task space while following a desired trajectory needs to be included. For simplicity, we will omit such kind of tasks in this book chapter.

with $\mathbf{F}(\mathbf{q}, \dot{\mathbf{q}}) = \mathbf{C}(\mathbf{q}, \dot{\mathbf{q}}) + \mathbf{G}(\mathbf{q}) + \varepsilon(\mathbf{q}, \dot{\mathbf{q}})$, and the notation $\mathbf{D}^+$ defining the pseudo inverse of a matrix such that $\mathbf{D}^+\mathbf{D} = \mathbf{I}$, $\mathbf{D}\mathbf{D}^+ = \mathbf{I}$, and with the matrix root $\mathbf{D}^{1/2}$ defined as $\mathbf{D}^{1/2}\mathbf{D}^{1/2} = \mathbf{D}$.

For example, the resolved-acceleration controller of Hsu et al. (Hsu et al., 1989) (without null space optimization) is the result of using the metric $\mathbf{N} = \mathbf{M}^{-2}$, which yields $\mathbf{u} = \mathbf{M}\mathbf{J}^T(\ddot{\mathbf{x}}_{\text{ref}} - \dot{\mathbf{J}}\dot{\mathbf{q}}) + \mathbf{F}$, and corresponds to a cascade of an inverse dynamics and an inverse kinematics control law. Another example is Khatib's formulation of operational space control (Khatib, 1987), determined by the metric $\mathbf{N} = \mathbf{M}^{-1}$ and given by

$$\mathbf{u} = \mathbf{J}^T(\mathbf{J}\mathbf{M}^{-1}\mathbf{J}^T)^{-1}(\ddot{\mathbf{x}}_{\text{ref}} - \dot{\mathbf{J}}\dot{\mathbf{q}} + \mathbf{J}\mathbf{M}^{-1}\mathbf{F}). \tag{3.5}$$

Khatib's solution is special as the metric $\mathbf{N} = \mathbf{M}^{-1}$ is the only metric which generated torques that correspond to the ones created by a physical contraint pulling the robot along the trajectory (Udwadia & Kalaba, 1996; Peters et al., 2005), i.e., it is the metric used by nature according to Gauss' principle (Bruyninckx & Khatib, 2000; Udwadia & Kalaba, 1996) and it is invariant under change of joint coordinates (Doty et al., 1993). Other metrics such as $\mathbf{N} = \text{const}$ can be used to distribute the required forces differently, e.g., such that stronger motors get a higher portion of the generated forces (Peters et al., 2005).

Even when achieving the task perfectly, the joint-space trajectories can result in unfavorable postures or even joint-space instability (see Example 3.1). For handling such cases, additional controls which do not affect the tasks performance but ensure a favorable joint-space behavior need to be included. From the point of view of the optimization framework, we would select a nominal control law $\mathbf{u}_0$ (e.g., a force which pulls the robot towards a rest posture $\mathbf{u}_0 = -\mathbf{K}_D\dot{\mathbf{q}} - \mathbf{K}_D(\mathbf{q} - \mathbf{q}_{\text{rest}})$), and then solve the constrained optimization problem

$$\min_{\mathbf{u}} C_1(\mathbf{u}) = (\mathbf{u} - \mathbf{u}_0)^T \mathbf{N}(\mathbf{u} - \mathbf{u}_0) \text{ s.t. } \mathbf{J}\ddot{\mathbf{q}} = \ddot{\mathbf{x}}_{\text{ref}} - \dot{\mathbf{J}}\dot{\mathbf{q}}, \tag{3.6}$$

where $\mathbf{u}_1 = \mathbf{u} - \mathbf{u}_0$ as the task-space control component. The general solution is given by

$$\begin{aligned}\mathbf{u} &= \mathbf{N}^{-1/2}(\mathbf{J}\mathbf{M}^{-1}\mathbf{N}^{-1/2})^+(\ddot{\mathbf{x}}_{\text{ref}} - \dot{\mathbf{J}}\dot{\mathbf{q}} + \mathbf{J}\mathbf{M}^{-1}\mathbf{F}) \\ &\quad + \mathbf{N}^{-1/2}(\mathbf{I} - (\mathbf{N}^{-1/2}\mathbf{M}^{-1}\mathbf{J})(\mathbf{J}\mathbf{M}^{-1}\mathbf{N}^{-1/2})^+)\mathbf{N}^{1/2}\mathbf{u}_0,\end{aligned} \tag{3.7}$$

where the second summand fulfill the nominal control law $\mathbf{u}_0$ in the null-space of the first term. When having more than two tasks, these can be nested in a similar fashion leading to a general framework of hierarchical task control (Peters et al., 2005; Sentis & Khatib, 2005).

Example 3.1 *An illustrative example of operational space control is tracking the end-effector position $x = q_1 + q_2$ of a prismatic robot with two parallel links with joint positions q_1, q_2, see Figure 3.1. The mass matrix will by $\mathbf{M} = \text{diag}(m_1, 0) + m_2\mathbf{1}$ with masses $m_1 = m_2 = 1$ and $\mathbf{1}$ denoting a matrix with all coefficients equal to one.*

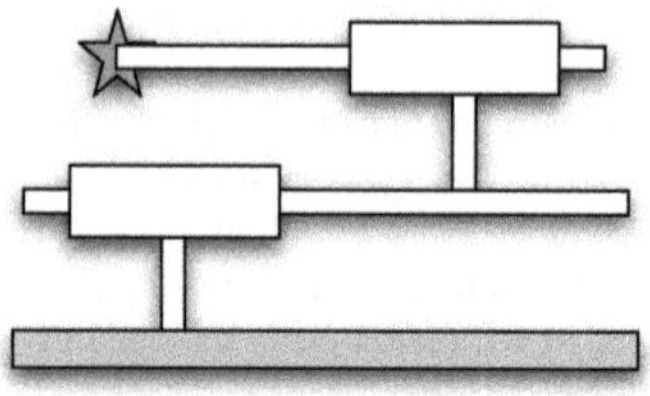

(a) Prismatic 2-dof robot

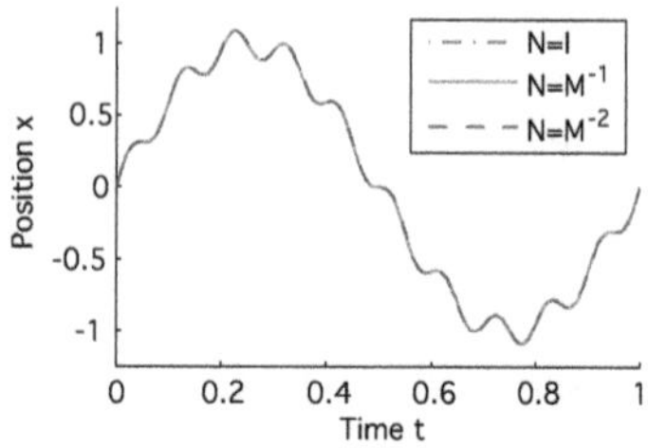

(b) End-effector position (all trajectories coincide almost perfectly with the refrence trajectory) x

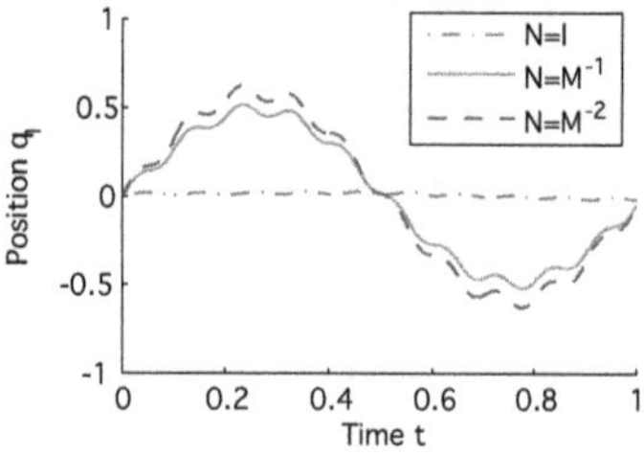

(c) Joint position q_1

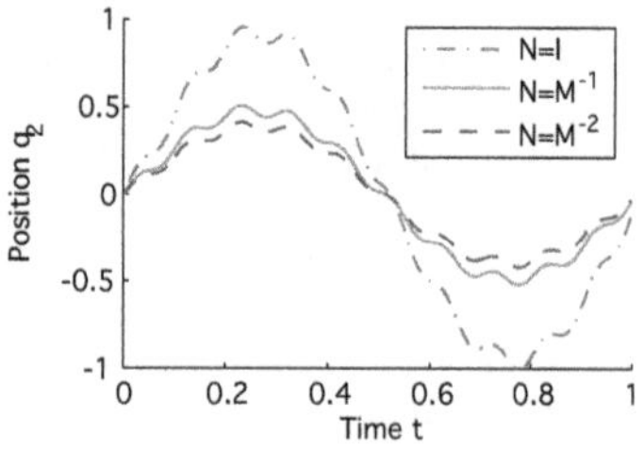

(d) Joint position q_2

Figure 3.1: When applied to the prismatic robot from Example 3.1 shown in (a), the three control laws for the metrics $\mathbf{N} = \mathbf{I}$ (dashed-dot red lines), $\mathbf{N} = \mathbf{M}^{-1}$ (solid green), $\mathbf{N} = \mathbf{M}^{-2}$ (dashed blue) result in (b) the same task-space tracking but (c,d) very different joint-space behavior. See Example 3.1 for more information.

The internal forces are $\mathbf{F} = 0$, the Jacobian is $\mathbf{J} = [1, 1]^T$ and its derivative $\dot{\mathbf{J}} = \mathbf{0}$. If no joint-space control law is selected, i.e., $\mathbf{u}_0 = 0$, the control law in the form of Equation (3.4) for executing the task $\ddot{x}_{ref} = \ddot{x}_d + K_d(\dot{x}_d - \dot{x}) + K_p(x_d - x)$ would result in unstable behavior for most metrics $\mathbf{N}$. When adding a $\mathbf{u}_0 = -\mathbf{K}_D\dot{\mathbf{q}} - \mathbf{K}_D\mathbf{q}$ pulling the robot towards $\mathbf{q}_{rest} = 0$, we obtain stable tracking with very different properties as can be observed in Figure 3.1: (i) metric $\mathbf{N} = \mathbf{I}$ will result in the second link tracking the end-effector and the null-space component stabilizing the first link, (ii) metric $\mathbf{N} = \mathbf{M}^{-1}$ will distribute the task on both links evenly and have the null-space component decouple the two links, while (iii) metric $\mathbf{N} = \mathbf{M}^{-2}$ simply minimizes the squared acceleration.

We will use this simple robot example (Example 3.1) to illustrate various other issues below as it allows easy analytical understanding and graphical visualizations.

3.1.3 Why should we learn Operational Space Control?

When an accurate analytical model of the robot is available and its parameters can be well-estimated, operational space control laws can be highly successful (Khatib, 1987; Sentis & Khatib, 2005; Nakanishi et al., 2005). However, in many new complex robotic systems, e.g., humanoid robots, space robots, etc., accurate analytical models of the robot dynamics are not available due to significant depatures from idealized theoretical models such as rigid body dynamics. For instance, in our experience with anthropomorphic robots, unmodeled nonlinear effects were caused by complex actuator dynamics, hydraulic hoses and cable bundles routed along the light weight structure of the robot as well as complex friction effects. Trying to model such nonlinearities is of little use due to the lack of generality of such an approach, and the daunting task of deriving useful models for the unknown effects.

Example 3.2 *In the prismatic robot from Example 3.1, already small unmodeled nonlinearities can have a drastic effect. If the estimated mass matrix of the robot* $\tilde{\mathbf{M}} = \mathrm{diag}\,(m_1, 0) + m_2\mathbf{1}$*(where* $\mathbf{1}$ *is a matrix with only ones as entries) just differs from the true* $\mathbf{M}$ *by* $M_{12} - \tilde{M}_{12} = M_{21} - \tilde{M}_{21} = 0.5 \sin{(q_1 + q_2)}$*, e.g., through unmodeled properties of cables, then the resulting control law will result in unstable and unpredictable null-space behavior despite that accurate task space tracking is theoretically still possible. On a real physical system, excessive null space behavior saturates the motors of the robot, such that also task space tracking degrades, and the entire control system goes unstable.*

Example 3.2 demonstrates how a small modeling error decreases the performance of the operational control law and can result in joint-space instability even for simple robots. For light-weight robot arms or full-body humanoid robots, such problems become even more frequent and difficult to cope with. Traditionally, this problem is be fixed by the engineer improving the approximation the plant by hand; however, for operational space control of low-gain controlled light-weight robots which are hard to model, learning is a promising novel alternative and will be discussed in Section 3.2.

3.2 Learning Methods for Operational Space Control

Learning operational space control with redundant manipulators is largely an unexplored problem and the literature has only few related examples. Among those, learning approaches to task level control focussed mostly on an inverse kinematics end-effector control (Guez & Ahmad, 1988; Jordan & Rumelhart, 1992; Bullock, Grossberg, & Guenther, 1993; Tevatia & Schaal, 2000; D'Souza, Vijayakumar, & Schaal, 2001), i.e., learning an inverse kinematics mapping, in order to create appropriate reference trajectories in joint-space, which were to be executed by a given joint-space control law or were simply optimizing a certain trajectory (De Luca & Mataloni, 1991). The combination of a learned inverse kinematics and a learned inverse dynamics controller (Guez & Ahmad,

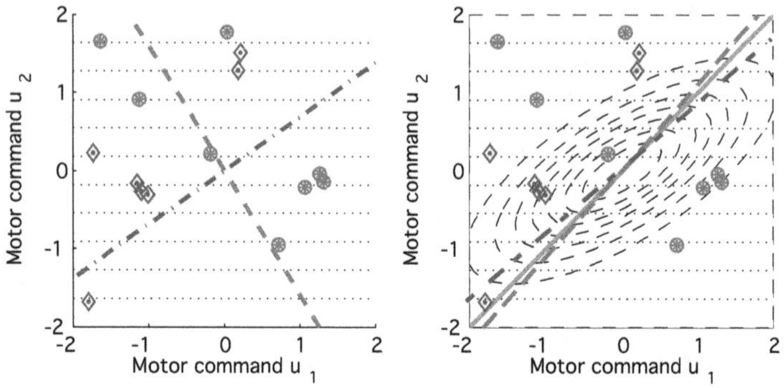

(a) Unweighted datasets

(b) Reward weighted datasets

Figure 3.2: This figure illustrates how (a) different data sets result in different solutions if each data point is treated with equal importance (the blue dash-dot line corresponds to the blue diamonds and the red dashed line to the red circles). If these data points are (b) weighted down using the Gaussian cost function (here indicated with the metric $\mathbf{N} = \mathbf{M}^{-1}$ as solid thin black lines) the solutions of different data sets will consistently approximate optimal solutions shown in the solid cyan line. While for the linear prismatic robot one could live with any solution in (a), different local solutions have to create a consistent global solution for nonlinear robots. The horizontal faintly dotted lines in (a) and (b) indicate contour lines of equal task-space acceleration.

1988; Tevatia & Schaal, 2000; D'Souza et al., 2001) can only be found occasionally in the literature. To the best of our knowledge, full operational space control laws with redundancy have not been addressed by general learning approaches to date.

3.2.1 Can Operational Space Control be learned?

Learning operational space control is equivalent to obtaining a mapping $(\mathbf{q}, \dot{\mathbf{q}}, \ddot{\mathbf{x}}_{\text{ref}}) \rightarrow \mathbf{u}$ from sampled data using a function approximator. However, as the dimensionality of the task-space reference trajectory $\ddot{\mathbf{x}}_{\text{ref}}$ is lower than the one of motor command $\mathbf{u}$, there are infinitely many solutions for $\mathbf{u}$ for most joint positions $\mathbf{q}$, and joint velocities $\dot{\mathbf{q}}$. For the illustrative linear case in Example 3.2 without a null-space component, this mapping corresponds to a line in the plane of possible control laws as shown by the two lines in Figure 3.2(a).

A major problem arises in the case of a robot with rotary joints as the motor commands $\mathbf{u}$ achieving the same reference acceleration $\ddot{\mathbf{x}}_{\text{ref}}$ are no longer form a convex set, a problem first described in the context of learning inverse kinematics (D'Souza et al., 2001; Jordan & Rumelhart, 1992). Thus, when learning the inverse mapping $(\mathbf{q}, \dot{\mathbf{q}}, \ddot{\mathbf{x}}_{\text{ref}}) \rightarrow \mathbf{u}$, the learning algorithm will average over unconnected sets of the solutions which can result in invalid solutions to the learning problem. Therefore, the learning problem is ill-conditioned such that directly learning from samples with supervised learning techniques is not suitable.

Nevertheless, the convexity issues can be resolved by employing a spatially localized supervised learning system, which, in our case, needs to spatially localized based on both joint space position and velocity – such an approach was first introduced in the context of inverse kinematics learning (Bullock et al., 1993; D'Souza et al., 2001). The feasibility of this idea can be demonstrated simply by averaging over the combination of Equations (3.2) and (3.1) which yields that by averaging over the exact same spatial position $\mathbf{q}$, and velocity $\dot{\mathbf{q}}$, we have

$$\begin{aligned}\overline{\ddot{\mathbf{x}}} &= \langle \ddot{\mathbf{x}} \rangle = \left\langle \mathbf{J}\mathbf{M}^{-1}(\mathbf{u}+\mathbf{F}) + \dot{\mathbf{J}}\dot{\mathbf{q}} \right\rangle \\ &= \mathbf{J}\mathbf{M}^{-1}\langle \mathbf{u}+\mathbf{F}\rangle + \dot{\mathbf{J}}\dot{\mathbf{q}} = \mathbf{J}\mathbf{M}^{-1}(\overline{\mathbf{u}}+\mathbf{F}) + \dot{\mathbf{J}}\dot{\mathbf{q}},\end{aligned} \tag{3.8}$$

i.e., in the vicinity of same $\mathbf{q}$,$\dot{\mathbf{q}}$, a particular $\overline{\ddot{\mathbf{x}}}$ will always correspond to exactly one particular $\overline{\mathbf{u}}$ [2]. Therefore, locally linear controllers

$$\mathbf{u}^i = \mathbf{c}^i_{\boldsymbol{\beta}}(\mathbf{q}, \dot{\mathbf{q}}, \ddot{\mathbf{x}}_{\text{ref}}) = [\ddot{\mathbf{x}}^T_{\text{ref}}, \dot{\mathbf{q}}^T, 1]\boldsymbol{\beta}^i, \tag{3.9}$$

can be used if they are only active in a region around $\mathbf{q}, \dot{\mathbf{q}}$ (note that we added constant input in Equation (3.9) to account for the intercept of a linear function). From a control engineering point of view, this argument corresponds to the insight that when we can linearize the plant in a certain region, we can find a local control law in that region by treating the plant as linear, and, in general, linear system do not have the problem of non-convexity of the solution space when learning an inverse function.

Next we need to address how to find an appropriate piecewise linearization for the locally linear controllers. For this purpose, we learn a locally linear forward or predictor model

$$\ddot{\mathbf{x}}^i = \mathbf{p}^i_{\hat{\boldsymbol{\beta}}}(\mathbf{q}, \dot{\mathbf{q}}, \mathbf{u}) = [\dot{\mathbf{q}}^T, \mathbf{u}^T, 1]\hat{\boldsymbol{\beta}}^i, \tag{3.10}$$

Learning this forward model is a standard supervised learning problem, as the mapping is guaranteed to be a proper function. A method of learning such a forward model that automatically also learns a local linearization is Locally Weighted Projection Regression (LWPR) (Schaal, Atkeson, & Vijayakumar, 2002), a fast online learning method which scales into high-dimensions, has been used for inverse dynamics control of humanoid robots, and can automatically determine the number of local models that are needed to

[2] Note, that the localization in velocity $\dot{\mathbf{q}}$ can be dropped for a pure rigid body formulation as it is linear in the $\dot{q}_i\dot{q}_j$ for all degrees of freedom i, j; this, however, is not necessarily desirable as it will add new inputs to the local regression problem which grows quadratically with the number of degrees of freedom.

represent the function. The membership to a local model is determined by a weight generated from a Gaussian kernel:

$$w^i(\mathbf{q}, \dot{\mathbf{q}}) = \exp\left(\frac{1}{2}\left(\begin{bmatrix}\mathbf{q}\\ \dot{\mathbf{q}}\end{bmatrix} - \mathbf{c}_i\right)^T \mathbf{D}^i \left(\begin{bmatrix}\mathbf{q}\\ \dot{\mathbf{q}}\end{bmatrix} - \mathbf{c}_i\right)\right) \qquad (3.11)$$

centered at $\mathbf{c}_i$ in $(\mathbf{q}, \dot{\mathbf{q}})$-space, and shaped by a distance metric $\mathbf{D}_i$. For a closer description of this statistical learning algorithm see (Schaal et al., 2002).

For each local forward model created by LWPR, we automatically create a local controller. This approach of pair-wise combining predictors and controllers is related by the MOSAIC architecture (Haruno, Wolpert, & Kawato, 1999) where the quality of predicting a task is used for selecting which local controller should be used for the task.

3.2.2 Combining the Local Controllers and Ensuring Consistent Resolution of Redundancy

In order to control a robot with these local control laws, they need to be combined into a consistent global control law. The combination is given by a weighted average (Schaal et al., 2002):

$$\mathbf{u} = \frac{\sum_{i=1}^{n} w^i(\mathbf{q}, \dot{\mathbf{q}})\,[\ddot{\mathbf{x}}_{\text{ref}}^T, \dot{\mathbf{q}}^T, 1]\boldsymbol{\beta}^i}{\sum_{i=1}^{n} w^i(\mathbf{q}, \dot{\mathbf{q}})}, \qquad (3.12)$$

where each control law $\mathbf{c}^i_{\beta}(\mathbf{q}, \dot{\mathbf{q}}, \ddot{\mathbf{x}}_{\text{ref}})$ is just valid in its local region computed by $w^i(\mathbf{q}, \dot{\mathbf{q}})$, and $\boldsymbol{\beta}^i$ are the parameters of each local operational space control law.

However, while the mappings $(\mathbf{q}, \dot{\mathbf{q}}, \ddot{\mathbf{x}}_{\text{ref}}) \rightarrow \mathbf{u}$ can properly be learned locally in the neighborhood of some $\mathbf{q}$,$\dot{\mathbf{q}}$, due to the redundancy in the robotic system, there is no guarantee that across the local mappings the same type of solution is acquired. This problem is due to the dependence of the inverse solution on the training data distribution in each local model – i.e., different distributions will pick different solutions for the inverse mapping from the infinity of possible inverses. In Figure 3.2 (a), we demonstrate this effect. While this problem is not devastating for the prismatic robot from Example 3.1, it is results in severe problems for any nonlinear robot requiring multiple, consistent linear models. There are two different approaches to tackling such problems: (1) by biasing the system towards using a pre-processed data set such that it can only produce one particular inverse solution (D'Souza et al., 2001), and (2) by incorporating a cost/reward function in order to favor a certain kind of solution (an example which will be discussed later and is shown Figure 3.2 (b)). The first approach lacks generality and can bias the learning system such that the task is not properly accomplished anymore. The major shortcoming of the second approach is that the choice of the cost/reward function is in general non-trivial and determines the learning algorithm as well as the learned solution.

The crucial component to finding a principled approach to this inconsistency problem is based on the discussion in Section 3.1.2 and previous work (Peters et al., 2005).

Operational space control can be seen as a constrained optimization problem with a cost function given in Equation (3.3). Thus, the cost function based approach for the creation of a consistent set of local controllers for operational space control can be based on this insight. The cost function can be turned into a immediate reward $r(\mathbf{u})$ by running it through an exponential function:

$$r(\mathbf{u}) = \sigma \exp\left(-0.5\sigma^2 C_1(\mathbf{u})\right) = \sigma \exp\left(-\sigma^{-2}\mathbf{u}_1^T \mathbf{N} \mathbf{u}_1\right), \tag{3.13}$$

where σ is a scaling factor and the task space command $\mathbf{u}_1 = \mathbf{u} - \mathbf{u}_0$ can be computed using a desired null-space behavior $\mathbf{u}_0$ (e.g., pulling towards a rest posture as discussed in Section 3.1.2). The scaling factor σ does not affect the optimality of a solution $\mathbf{u}$ as it acts as a monotonic transformation in this cost function. However, it can increase the efficiency of the learning algorithm significantly when only sparse data is available for learning (i.e., as for most interesting robots as the high-dimensional action spaces of complex robots will hardly ever be filled densely with data)[3]. These local rewards allow us the reformulation of our learning problem as an *immediate reward reinforcement learning problem* (Dayan & Hinton, 1997), as will be discussed in Section 3.3.

We are now in the position to formulate a supervised learning algorithm for the local operational space controllers. The task constraint in Equation (3.3) as well as the rigid body dynamics in Equation (3.1) are automatically fulfilled by all data sampled from the real robot similar to a self-supervised learning problem. Therefore, for learning the local operational space controllers, we have obtained a local linear regression problem where we attempt to learn primarily from the observed motor commands $\mathbf{u}^k$ which also have a high reward $r(\mathbf{u}^k)$ within each active local model $\mathbf{c}^i_\beta(\mathbf{q}^k, \dot{\mathbf{q}}^k, \ddot{\mathbf{x}}^k_{\text{ref}})$. An intuitive solution is to use reward-weighted regression, i.e., find the solution which minimizes

$$\sum_{k=1}^{N} r\left(\mathbf{u}^k\right) w^i\left(\mathbf{q}^k, \dot{\mathbf{q}}^k\right)\left(\mathbf{u}^k - [\ddot{\mathbf{x}}^{k,T}_{\text{ref}}, \dot{\mathbf{q}}^{k,T}, 1]\boldsymbol{\beta}^i\right)^2 \rightarrow \min, \tag{3.14}$$

for each controller i. The solution to this problem is the well-known weighted regression formula:

$$\boldsymbol{\beta} = \left(\boldsymbol{\Phi}^T \mathbf{W} \boldsymbol{\Phi}\right)^{-1} \boldsymbol{\Phi}^T \mathbf{W} \mathbf{U}, \tag{3.15}$$

with rows in the matrices $\boldsymbol{\Phi}$ and $\mathbf{U}$: $\boldsymbol{\Phi}_k = [\ddot{\mathbf{x}}^{k,T}_{\text{ref}}, \dot{\mathbf{q}}^{k,T}, 1]$, $\mathbf{U}_k = \mathbf{u}^{k,T}$ and $\mathbf{W}_i = r\left(\mathbf{u}^i\right) w(\mathbf{q}^i, \dot{\mathbf{q}}^i)$. When employing this reward-weighted regression solution, we will converge to a globally consistent solution across all local controllers. The learning algorithm is shown in Table 3.1 together with an additional component derived in Section 3.3. Note that this step was only possible due to the essential cost function in Equation (3.6) from our previous work.

[3]The reward has to be seen in the light of the relationship between the Gaussian distribution and Gauss' principle for constrained motion as suggested already by Carl-Friedrich Gauss in his original work(Udwadia, 2005).

Algorithm: Learning for Operational Space Control

for each new data point $[\ddot{\mathbf{x}}^k_{\text{ref}}, \mathbf{q}, \dot{\mathbf{q}}^k, \mathbf{u}^k]$
  Add $(\mathbf{q}, \dot{\mathbf{q}}, \mathbf{u}) \rightarrow \ddot{\mathbf{x}}$ to the forward model regression.
  Determine the current number of models n and
  localizations of the forward models $w^i(\mathbf{q}, \dot{\mathbf{q}})$.
  Compute desired null-space behavior $\mathbf{u}^k_0 = f\left(\mathbf{q}^k, \dot{\mathbf{q}}^k\right)$.
  Compute costs $C^k_1 = \left(\mathbf{u}^k_1\right)^T \mathbf{N}\left(\mathbf{q}^k\right) \mathbf{u}^k_1$ with $\mathbf{u}^k_1 = \mathbf{u}^k - \mathbf{u}^k_0$.
  For each model $i = 1, 2, \ldots, n$
    Update mean cost:
    $\sigma^2_i = \sum_{h=1}^{k} w^k\left(\mathbf{q}^h, \dot{\mathbf{q}}^h\right) C^k_1 \Big/ \sum_{k=1}^{N} w^k\left(\mathbf{q}^h, \dot{\mathbf{q}}^h\right)$,
    Compute reward:
    $r(\mathbf{u}) = \sigma_i \exp\left(-0.5\sigma^2_i C^k_1\right)$
    Add data point to weighted regression so that:
    $\mathbf{\Phi}_i = [\mathbf{q}^i, \dot{\mathbf{q}}^i, \ddot{\mathbf{x}}^i_{\text{ref}}]$
    $\mathbf{U}_i = \mathbf{u}^i$
    $\mathbf{W} = \operatorname{diag}\left(r(\mathbf{u}^1) w^1, \ldots, r(\mathbf{u}^n) w^n\right)$
    Perform policy update by regression
    $\beta_{k+1} = \left(\mathbf{\Phi}^T \mathbf{W} \mathbf{\Phi}\right)^{-1} \mathbf{\Phi}^T \mathbf{W} \mathbf{U}$,
  end
end

Table 3.1: This table shows the complete learning algorithm for Operational Space Control. See text of detailed explanations.

3.3 Reformulation as Reinforcement Learning Problem

Another way of looking at operational space control is to view it as an immediate reward reinforcement learning problem (Kaebling, Littman, & Moore, 1996) with high-dimensional, continuous states $\mathbf{s} = [\mathbf{q}, \dot{\mathbf{q}}, \ddot{\mathbf{x}}_{\text{ref}}, \mathbf{u}_0] \in \mathbb{R}^n$ and actions $\mathbf{u} \in \mathbb{R}^m$. The goal of learning is to obtain an optimal policy

$$\mathbf{u} = \mu\left(\mathbf{q}, \dot{\mathbf{q}}, \ddot{\mathbf{x}}_{\text{ref}}, \mathbf{u}_0\right) = \mu\left(\mathbf{s}\right) \tag{3.16}$$

such that the system follows the reference acceleration $\ddot{\mathbf{x}}_{\text{ref}}$ while maximizing the immediate reward $r\left(\mathbf{u}\right) = -(\mathbf{u} - \mathbf{u}_0)^T\mathbf{N}(\mathbf{u} - \mathbf{u}_0)$ for any given nominal behavior $\mathbf{u}_0$. In order to incorporate exploration during learning, we need a stochastic control policy $\mathbf{u} = \mu_{\boldsymbol{\theta}}(\mathbf{q}, \dot{\mathbf{q}}, \ddot{\mathbf{x}}_{\text{ref}}) + \varepsilon$, modeled as a probability distribution $\pi_{\boldsymbol{\theta}}(\mathbf{u}|\mathbf{s}) = p(\mathbf{u}|\mathbf{s}, \boldsymbol{\theta})$ with parameter vector $\boldsymbol{\theta}$. The goal of the learning system is thus to find the policy parameters $\boldsymbol{\theta}$ that maximize

$$J_r\left(\boldsymbol{\theta}\right) = \int p\left(\mathbf{s}\right) \int \pi_{\boldsymbol{\theta}}\left(\mathbf{u}|\mathbf{s}\right) r\left(\mathbf{s}, \mathbf{u}\right) d\mathbf{u} d\mathbf{s}. \tag{3.17}$$

$p(\mathbf{s})$ denotes the distribution of states, which is treated as fixed in immediate reward reinforcement learning problems (Kaebling et al., 1996).

Originally, we derived this algorithm from a weighted regression point of view. However, this point of view is not completely satisfying as it still has the open parameter σ^2 which determines the speed of convergence of the learning controllers. An alternative view point, i.e., in the framework of immediate reward reinforcement learning, allows deriving the previous algorithm together with a computation rule for σ^2. Previous work in the literature suggested a variety of optimizing methods which can be applied to immediate reward reinforcement learning problems, e.g., gradient based methods (e.g., REINFORCE, Covariant REINFORCE, finite difference gradients, the Kiefer-Wolfowitz procedure, A_{RP} algorithms, CRBP, etc.) and random search algorithms (e.g., simulated annealing or genetic algorithms) (Dayan & Hinton, 1997; Kaebling et al., 1996; Spall, 2003). However, gradient-based methods tend to be too slow for the online learning that we desire in our problem, while randomized search algorithms can create too arbitrary solutions, often not suitable for execution on a robotic system. For learning operational space control, we require a method that is computationally sufficiently efficient to deal with high-dimensional robot systems and large amounts of data, that has a low sample complexity, that comes with convergence guarantees, and that is suitable for smooth online improvement. For instance, linear regression techniques and/or methods employing EM-style algorithms are highly desirable.

A good starting point for our work is the probabilistic reinforcement learning framework by Dayan & Hinton (1997). As we will show in the following, a generalization of this approach allows us to derive an EM-algorithm which essentially reduces the immediate reward learning problem to a reward-weighted regression problem.

3.3.1 Reward Transformation

In order to maximize the expected return (Equation 3.17) using samples, we approximate

$$J_r(\boldsymbol{\theta}) \approx \sum\nolimits_{i=1}^{n} \pi_{\boldsymbol{\theta}}(\mathbf{u}_i|\mathbf{s}_i)\, r_i \tag{3.18}$$

where $r_i = r(\mathbf{s}_i, \mathbf{u}_i)$. For application of the probabilistic reinforcement learning framework of Dayan & Hinton (Dayan & Hinton, 1997), the reward needs to be strictly positive such that it resembles an (improper) probability distribution. While this can be achieved by a linear rescaling for problems for bounded rewards, for unbounded rewards as discussed in this paper, a nonlinear transformation of the reward $U_{\tau}(r)$ is required, with the constraint that the optimal solution to the underlying problem remains unchanged. Thus, we require that $U_{\tau}(r)$ is strictly monotonic with respect to r, and additionally that $U_{\tau}(r) \geq 0$ and $\int_0^{\infty} U_{\tau}(r)\, dr = \text{const}$, resulting in the transformed optimization problem

$$J_u(\boldsymbol{\theta}) = \sum\nolimits_{i=1}^{n} \pi_{\boldsymbol{\theta}}(\mathbf{u}_i|\mathbf{s}_i)\, U_{\tau}(r_i)\,. \tag{3.19}$$

The reward transformation plays a more important role than initially meets the eye: as already pointed out in (Dayan & Hinton, 1997), convergence speed can be greatly affected by this transformation. Making $U_{\tau}(r)$ an adaptive part of the learning algorithm by means of some internal parameters $\boldsymbol{\tau}$ can greatly accelerate the learning speed and help avoid local minima during learning. Figure 3.3 demonstrates this issue with a 1D continuous state and 1D continuous action example, where the goal is to learn an optimal linear policy. Using the algorithm that we will introduce below, an adaptive reward transformation accelerated the convergence by a factor of 4, and actually significantly helped avoiding local minima during learning.

3.3.2 EM Reinforcement Learning with Reward Transformation

To derive our learning algorithm, similar as in (Dayan & Hinton, 1997), we start by establishing the lower bound

$$\log J_u(\boldsymbol{\theta}) = \log \sum\nolimits_{i=1}^{n} q(i)\, \frac{\pi_{\boldsymbol{\theta}}(\mathbf{u}_i|\mathbf{s}_i)\, U_{\tau}(r_i)}{q(i)} \tag{3.20}$$

$$\geq \sum\nolimits_{i=1}^{n} q(i) \log \frac{\pi_{\boldsymbol{\theta}}(\mathbf{u}_i|\mathbf{s}_i)\, U_{\tau}(r_i)}{q(i)} \tag{3.21}$$

$$= \sum\nolimits_{i=1}^{n} q(i) \left[\log \pi_{\boldsymbol{\theta}}(\mathbf{u}_i|\mathbf{s}_i) + \log U_{\tau}(r_i) - \log q(i)\right] \tag{3.22}$$

$$= \mathcal{F}(q, \boldsymbol{\theta}, \boldsymbol{\tau})\,, \tag{3.23}$$

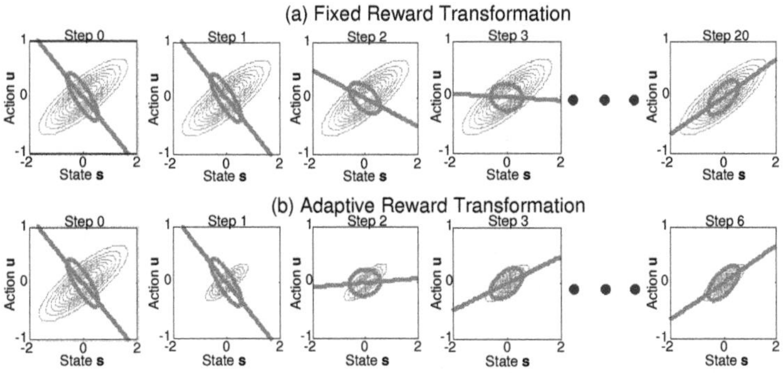

Figure 3.3: A comparison of fixed and adaptive reward transformation for learning a linear policy $\pi(u|s) = \mathcal{N}(u|\theta_1 s + \theta_2, \sigma^2)$ under the transformed reward $u(r(s,u)) = \exp(-\tau(q_1 u^2 + q_2 us + sq_3^2))$. The transformed reward is indicated by the dotted blue ellipses, the variance of the action distribution is indicated by the red thick ellipse, and the mean of the linear policy is shown by the red thick line. With τ being adaptive, significantly faster learning of the optimal policy is achieved. Step 0 shows the initial policy and initial transformed reward, Step 1 shows the initial policy with adapted transformed reward.

due to Jensens inequality. The re-weighting distribution $q(i)$ obeys the constraint

$$\sum\nolimits_{i=1}^{n} q(i) - 1 = 0. \tag{3.24}$$

The resulting EM algorithm is given below.

Algorithm 3.1 *An EM algorithm for optimizing both the expected reward as well as the reward-transformation is given by an* ***E-Step***

$$q_{k+1}(j) = \frac{\pi_{\boldsymbol{\theta}_k}(\mathbf{u}_j|\mathbf{s}_j)\, U_{\tau_k}(r_j)}{\sum_{i=1}^{n} \pi_{\boldsymbol{\theta}}(\mathbf{u}_i|\mathbf{s}_i)\, U_{\tau_k}(r_i)}, \tag{3.25}$$

an ***M-Step*** *for the policy parameter update given*

$$\boldsymbol{\theta}_{k+1} = \arg\max_{\boldsymbol{\theta}} \sum\nolimits_{i=1}^{n} q_{k+1}(i) \log \pi_{\boldsymbol{\theta}}(\mathbf{u}_i|\mathbf{s}_i), \tag{3.26}$$

and a ***M-Step*** *for the adaptive reward transformation given by*

$$\boldsymbol{\tau}_{k+1} = \arg\max_{\boldsymbol{\tau}} \sum\nolimits_{i=1}^{n} q_{k+1}(i) \log U_{\boldsymbol{\tau}}(r_i). \tag{3.27}$$

Proof. The E-Step is given by

$$q_{k+1} = \arg\max_{q} \mathcal{F}(q, \boldsymbol{\theta}, \boldsymbol{\tau}) \tag{3.28}$$

while fulfilling the constraint

$$0 = \sum\nolimits_{i=1}^{n} q(i) - 1. \tag{3.29}$$

Thus, we obtain a constrained optimization problem with Lagrange multiplier λ:

$$L(\lambda, q) = \sum\nolimits_{i=1}^{n} q(i) \left[\log \pi_{\boldsymbol{\theta}}(\mathbf{u}_i|\mathbf{s}_i) + \log U_\tau(r_i) - \log q(i) + \lambda\right] - \lambda. \tag{3.30}$$

Optimizing $L(\lambda, q)$ with respect to q and λ results in Equation (3.25). Optimizing $\mathcal{F}(q_{k+1}, \boldsymbol{\theta}, \boldsymbol{\tau})$ with respect to θ and τ yields Equations(3.26, 3.27). ■

3.3.3 Reinforcement Learning by Reward-Weighted Regression

Let us assume the specific class of normally distributed policies:

$$\pi_{\boldsymbol{\theta}}(\mathbf{u}|\mathbf{s}) = \mathcal{N}\left(\mathbf{u}|\mu_\theta(\mathbf{s}), \sigma^2\mathbf{I}\right) \tag{3.31}$$

with a nominal or mean behavior $\mu_{\boldsymbol{\theta}}(\mathbf{s}) = \boldsymbol{\phi}(\mathbf{s})^T \boldsymbol{\theta}$ where $\boldsymbol{\phi}(\mathbf{s})$ denotes some fixed preprocessing of the state by basis functions and $\sigma^2\mathbf{I}$ determines the exploration[4]. Furthermore, we choose the reward transformation

$$U_\tau(r) = \tau \exp(-\tau r), \tag{3.32}$$

which, for $r > 0$ fulfills all our requirements on a reward transformation (cited from Sec.3.3.1). Algorithm 3.1 thus becomes:

Algorithm 3.2 *The update equations for the policy* $\pi_{\boldsymbol{\theta}}(\mathbf{u}|\mathbf{s}) = \mathcal{N}(\mathbf{u}|\mu_\theta(\mathbf{s}), \sigma^2\mathbf{I})$ *are:*

$$\boldsymbol{\theta}_{k+1} = \left(\boldsymbol{\Phi}^T\mathbf{W}\boldsymbol{\Phi}\right)^{-1}\boldsymbol{\Phi}^T\mathbf{W}\mathbf{Y}, \tag{3.33}$$

$$\sigma_{k+1}^2 = \left\|\mathbf{Y} - \boldsymbol{\theta}_{k+1}^T\boldsymbol{\Phi}\right\|_{\mathbf{W}}^2, \tag{3.34}$$

where

$$\mathbf{W} = \left(\sum_{i=1}^{n} U_\tau(r_i)\right)^{-1} \operatorname{diag}\left(U_\tau(r_1), U_\tau(r_2), \ldots, U_\tau(r_n)\right), \tag{3.35}$$

[4]Note that $\sigma^2\mathbf{I}$ could be replaced by a full variance matrix with little changes in the algorithm. However, this would result in a quadratic growth of parameters with the dimensionality of the state and is therefore less desirable.

denotes a diagonal matrix with transformed rewards,

$$\boldsymbol{\Phi} = [\boldsymbol{\phi}(\mathbf{s}_1), \boldsymbol{\phi}(\mathbf{s}_2), \ldots, \boldsymbol{\phi}(\mathbf{s}_n)]^T, \tag{3.36}$$

and

$$\mathbf{Y} = [\mathbf{u}_1, \mathbf{u}_2, \ldots, \mathbf{u}_n]^T \tag{3.37}$$

the motor commands. The update of the reward transformation $U_\tau(r) = \tau \exp(-\tau r)$ *is*

$$\tau_{k+1} = \frac{\sum_{i=1}^n U_{\tau_k}(r_i)}{\sum_{i=1}^n U_{\tau_k}(r_i) r_i}. \tag{3.38}$$

Proof. When computing $q_{k+1}(j)$ from samples in Equation (3.25), we have

$$q_{k+1}(j) = \frac{U_{\tau_k}(r_j)}{\sum_{i=1}^n U_{\tau_k}(r_i)} \tag{3.39}$$

as the probabilities are replaced by relative frequencies. We insert the policy

$$\pi_{\boldsymbol{\theta}}(\mathbf{u}|\mathbf{s}) = (2\pi\sigma^2)^{-\frac{d}{2}} \exp\left(-\frac{(\mathbf{u} - \boldsymbol{\phi}(\mathbf{s})^T\boldsymbol{\theta})^T(\mathbf{u} - \boldsymbol{\phi}(\mathbf{s})^T\boldsymbol{\theta})}{2\sigma^2}\right), \tag{3.40}$$

into Equation (3.26). By differentiating with respect to θ and equating the result to zero, we obtain

$$\boldsymbol{\theta} = \left(\sum_{i=1}^n q_{k+1}(i)\,\boldsymbol{\phi}(\mathbf{s}_i)\,\boldsymbol{\phi}(\mathbf{s}_i)^T\right)^{-1}\left(\sum_{i=1}^n q_{k+1}(i)\,\boldsymbol{\phi}(\mathbf{s}_i)\,\mathbf{u}_i\right). \tag{3.41}$$

In matrix vector form, this corresponds to Equation (3.33). Analogously, the reward transformation is obtained from differentiation with respect to τ as

$$\sum_{i=1}^n q_{k+1}(i)\frac{\partial}{\partial\tau}\log U_\tau(r_i) = \sum_{i=1}^n q_{k+1}(i)\left(\tau^{-1} - r_i\right) = 0. \tag{3.42}$$

which results in Equation (3.38). ■

3.4 Evaluations

We evaluated our approach on two different simulated, physically realistic robots: (i) a three degree-of-freedom (DOF) planar robot arm shown in Figure 3.4 (a) and (ii) a seven DOF simulated SARCOS master robot arm – an implementation on the real, physical SARCOS master robot arm (Figure 3.5 (a)) is currently in progress.

Both experiments were conducted as follows: first, learning the forward models and an initial control policy in each local model was obtained from random point-to-point

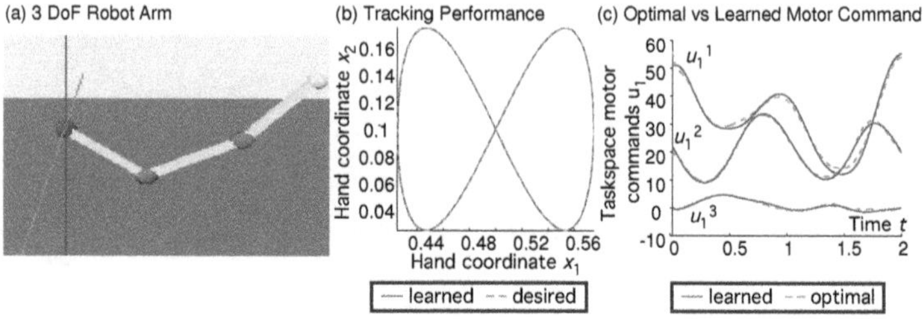

Figure 3.4: (a) screen shot of the 3 DOF arm simulator, (b) near ideal tracking performance for a planar figure-8 pattern for the 3 DOF arm, and (c) a comparison between the analytically obtained optimal control commands to the learned ones for one figure-8 cycle of the 3DOF arm exhibits that a near-optimal policy is obtained.

movements in joint space using a simple PD control law. This "motor babbling" exploration was necessary in order bootstrap learning with some initial data, as we would otherwise experience rather slow learning, as typically observed in similar direct-inverse learning approaches (Jordan & Rumelhart, 1992). The measured end-effector accelerations served as desired acceleration in Equation 3.9, and all other variables for learning the local controllers were measurable as well. Subsequently, the learning controller was used on-policy with the normally distributed actuator noise serving as exploration.

Both robots learned to track desired trajectories with high accuracy, as shown in Figures 3.4 (b) and 3.5 (b). For the three DOF arm, we verified the quality of the learned control commands in comparison to the analytical solution, given in Equation (3.7): Figure 3.4 (c) demonstrates that the motor commands of the learned and analytically optimal case are almost identical. Learning results of the simulated seven DOF Sarcos robot achieved almost the same end-effector tracking quality and is shown in Figure 3.4 (c). It exhibits only slightly increased errors, however, the joint commands were not quite as close to the optimal ones as for the 3 DOF arm – the rather high dimensional learning space of the 7 DOF arm most likely requires more extensive training and more careful tuning of the LWPR learning algorithm to achieve local linearizations with very high accuracy and with enough data to find the optimal solution. The 3 DOF required about 2 hours of real-time training, while setup was optimized for the 7 DOF arm where 60 minute run of real-time training was sufficient for achieving the quality exhibited on the test trajectory in Figure 3.5 (b).

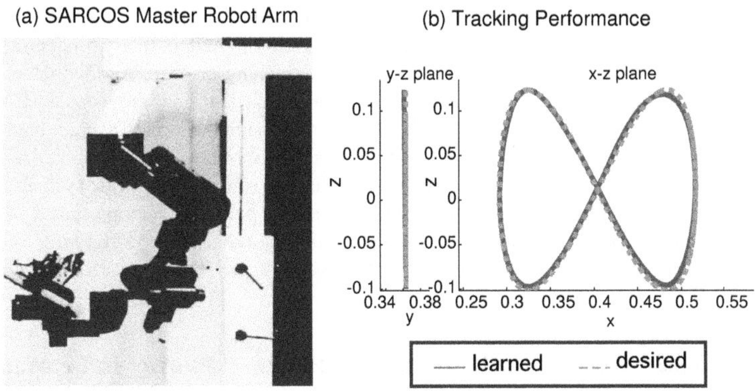

Figure 3.5: (a) Anthropomorphic Sarcos Master Arm, used as simulated system and in progress of actual robot evaluations. (b) Tracking performance for a planar figure-8 pattern for the simulated Sarcos Master arm.

3.5 Conclusion & Discussion

The contributions of this chapter are outlined in Section 3.5.1. The remaining open issue of non-constant metrics is discussed in Section 3.5.2.

3.5.1 Contributions of this Chapter

In this book chapter, a general learning framework for operational space for redundant robots has been presented, which is probably the first successful attempt of learning such control laws to date. We overcome the difficulties of having a non-convex data distribution by only learning in the vincinity of a local model anchored both in joint velocity and joint position. The local regions are obtained by learning forward models, which predict the movement of the end-effector. The global consistency of the redundancy resolution of the local model controllers is ensured through minimizing the cost function of operational space control. This cost function, derived in our previous work, is crucial to the success of this framework and its absence has most likely been the reason for the absence of learning operational space controllers to date. The resulting learning algorithm for the local models can be understood from two perspective, i.e., as a weighted regression problem where we intend to match the reward weighted motor commands (after transforming the cost into a reward) or as a reinforcement learning problem where we attempt to maximize an immediate reward criterion. Throughout this book chapter, we have illustrated the problems and advantages of learning operational space control using a prismatic two degrees of freedom robot arm as example. As application, we have shown a task-space trajectory following on a three degrees of freedom rotary robot arm, where we could exhibit near-perfect operational space tracking control. As robotics increasingly moves away from the structured domains of industrial robotics towards complex robotic systems, which both are increasingly high-dimensional and increasingly hard to model, such as humanoid robots, the techniques and theory developed in this book chapter will be beneficial in developing truly autonomous and self-tuning robotic systems.

The work presented in this chapter up to this point has been presented in (Peters & Schaal, 2006a, 2007a, 2007b) and the resulting journal paper is currently under review at the International Journal of Robotics Research (IJRR) for the IJRR Special Issue on Robot Learning.

3.5.2 Future Work: Using Intertia-based Metrics in Learning

In Section 2.5.2, we have seen that the inertia-based metrics have a particular importance as they do not require special null-space laws in order to be infinite horizon optimal. Thus, in order to learn the resulting important control laws known from analytical robotics, i.e., Khatib-Gauss (Khatib, 1987) and Hsu-IDM Control Laws (Hsu et al., 1989), our learning algorithm needs to be modified in order to be able to compute the appropriate rewards. In Section 3.3, we have assumed that the reward $r(\mathbf{u},\mathbf{q}) = \exp\left(-\mathbf{u}^T\mathbf{N}(\mathbf{q})\,\mathbf{u}\right)$ can be computed without difficulty which is the case, e.g., for $\mathbf{N}(\mathbf{q}) = \mathrm{const}$. However, this is not the case for metrics in the form $\mathbf{N}(\mathbf{q}) = \mathbf{M}^{-n}(\mathbf{q})$ as these require the exact determination of the expensive and error-prone inertia tensor. Therefore, when trying to learn an operational space controller with this kind of a metric, we would run into the same kind of difficulties as analytical approaches with modeling errors, or, at least, learn a different control law, which does not fully realize the interesting properties of the desired control law, e.g., the Khatib-Gauss control law. Nevertheless, through a reformulation of the learning problem, we can compute the reward without explicitly using the inertia tensor when employing a forward-inverse modeling approach similar to (Haruno et al., 1999). For this reformulation, we realize from Equation (3.1) that

$$\mathbf{M}^{-1}\mathbf{u}_1 = \ddot{\mathbf{q}} - \mathbf{M}^{-1}(\mathbf{F}+\mathbf{u}_0) = \ddot{\mathbf{q}} - \mathbf{g}_\beta(\mathbf{q},\dot{\mathbf{q}},\mathbf{u}_0) \equiv \boldsymbol{\delta}\ddot{\mathbf{q}}, \tag{3.43}$$

where $\ddot{\mathbf{q}} = \mathbf{g}_\beta(\mathbf{q},\dot{\mathbf{q}},\mathbf{u})$ denotes a learned forward model (or predictor) which predicts acceleration $\ddot{\mathbf{q}}$ for a given motor command $\mathbf{u} = \mathbf{u}_0 + \mathbf{u}_1$ at the joint positions $\mathbf{q}$ and velocities $\dot{\mathbf{q}}$. Using this motor command induced acceleration difference $\boldsymbol{\delta}\ddot{\mathbf{q}}$, we can determine the rewards for Khatib-Gauss and Hsu-IDM control laws by

$$r_{\mathrm{K}}(\mathbf{u}) = \exp(-\mathbf{u}_1^T\mathbf{M}^{-1}\mathbf{u}_1) = \exp(-\mathbf{u}_1^T\boldsymbol{\delta}\ddot{\mathbf{q}}), \tag{3.44}$$

$$r_{\mathrm{H}}(\mathbf{u}) = \exp(-\mathbf{u}_1^T\mathbf{M}^{-2}\mathbf{u}_1) = \exp(-\boldsymbol{\delta}\ddot{\mathbf{q}}^T\boldsymbol{\delta}\ddot{\mathbf{q}}), \tag{3.45}$$

respectively. This approach has been tested successfully on the prismatic robot, but requires further evaluation for interesting robot systems.

Chapter 4

Policy Gradient Methods for Motor Primitives and Robotics

Each problem that I solved became a rule
which served afterwards to solve other problems.
Rene Descartes (French philosopher and scientist, 1596-1650),

One of the major challenges in both action generation for robotics and in the understanding of human motor control is to learn the "building blocks of movement generation", called motor primitives. Motor primitives, as used in this book chapter, are parameterized control policies such as splines or nonlinear differential equations with desired attractor properties and correspond to the desired behaviours in the form $\mathbf{A}\ddot{\mathbf{x}} = \mathbf{b}$ which we have been using in the two preceeding chapters. While a lot of progress has been made in teaching parameterized motor primitives using supervised or imitation learning, the self-improvement by interaction of the system with the environment remains a challenging problem.

In this book chapter, we evaluate different reinforcement learning approaches for improving the performance of parameterized motor primitives. For pursuing this goal, we highlight the difficulties with current reinforcement learning methods, and outline both established and novel algorithms for the gradient-based improvement of parameterized policies. We compare these algorithms in the context of motor primitive learning, and show that our most modern algorithm, the Episodic Natural Actor-Critic outperforms previous algorithms by at least an order of magnitude. We demonstrate the efficiency of this reinforcement learning method in the application of learning to hit a baseball with an anthropomorphic robot arm.

4.1 Introduction

In order to ever leave the well-structured environments of factory floors and research labs, future robots will require the ability to aquire novel behaviors and motor skills as well as to improve existing ones based on rewards and costs. Similarly, the understanding of human motor control would benefit significantly if we can synthesize simulated human behavior and its underlying cost functions based on insight from machine learning and biological inspirations. Reinforcement learning is probably the most general framework in which such learning problems of computational motor control can be phrased. However, in order to bring reinforcement learning into the domain of human movement learning, two deciding components need to be added to the standard framework of reinforcement learning: first, we need a domain-specific policy representation for motor skills, and, second, we need reinforcement learning algorithms which work efficiently with this representation while scaling into the domain of high-dimensional mechanical systems such as humanoid robots.

Traditional representations of motor behaviors in robotics are mostly based on desired trajectories generated from spline interpolations between points, i.e., spline nodes, which are part of a longer sequence of intermediate target points on the way to a final movement goal. While such a representation is easy to understand, the resulting control policies, generated from a tracking controller of the spline trajectories, have a variety of significant disadvantages, including that they are time-indexed and thus not robust towards unforeseen disturbances, that they do not easily generalize to new bahavioral sitations without complete recomputing of the spline, and that they cannot easily be coordinated with other events in the environment, e.g., synchronized with other sensory variables like visual perception during catching a ball. In the literature, a variety of other approaches for parameterizing motor primitives have been suggested to overcome these problems, see (Ijspeert et al., 2002, 2003) for more information. One of these approaches proposed to use parameterized nonlinear dynamical systems as motor primitives, where the attractor properties of these dynamical systems defined the desired behavior (Ijspeert et al., 2002, 2003). The resulting framework was particularly well suited for supervised imitation learning in robotics, exemplified by examples from humanoid robotics where a full-body humanoid learned tennis swings or complex polyrhythmic drumming pattern. One goal of this book chapter is the application of reinforcement learning to both traditional spline-based representations as well as the more novel dynamic system based approach.

However, despite that reinforcement learning is the most general framework for discussing the learning of motor primitives for robotics, most of the methods proposed in the reinforcement learning community are not applicable to high-dimensional systems such as humanoid robots as these methods do not scale beyond systems with more than three or four degrees of freedom and/or cannot deal with parameterized policies. Policy gradient methods are a notable exception to this statement. Starting with the pioneering work[1] of Gullapali and colleagues (Benbrahim & Franklin, 1997; Gullapalli, Franklin, & Benbrahim, 1994) in the early 1990s, these methods have been applied to a variety of

[1]Note that there has been earlier work in the control community,see e.g., (Jacobson & Mayne, 1970; Dyer & McReynolds, 1970; Hasdorff, 1976)., which is based on exact analytical models. Extensions based on learned, approximate models originated in the public policy literature, see (Werbos, 1979), and have

robot learning problems ranging from simple control tasks (e.g., balancing a ball-on a beam (Benbrahim, Doleac, Franklin, & Selfridge, 1992) , and pole-balancing (Kimura & Kobayashi, 1998)) to complex learning tasks involving many degrees of freedom such as learning of complex motor skills (Peters et al., 2005; Peters & Schaal, 2006b; Miyamoto et al., 1995, 1996; Gullapalli et al., 1994; Mitsunaga, Smith, Kanda, Ishiguro, & Hagita, 2005) and locomotion (Kimura & Kobayashi, 1997; Sato, Nakamura, & Ishii, 2002; Kohl & Stone, 2004; Endo, Morimoto, Matsubara, Nakanishi, & Cheng, 2005; Tedrake, Zhang, & Seung, 2005; Mori, Nakamura, Sato, & Ishii, 2004; Nakamura, Mori, & Ishii, 2004).

The advantages of policy gradient methods for parameterized motor primitives are numerous. Among the most important ones are that the policy representation can be chosen such that it is meaningful for the task, i.e., we can use a suitable motor primitive representation, and that domain knowledge can be incorporated, which often leads to fewer parameters in the learning process in comparison to traditional value-function based approaches. Moreover, there exists a variety of different algorithms for policy gradient estimation in the literature, which have a rather strong theoretical underpinning. Additionally, policy gradient methods can be used model-free and therefore also be applied to problems without analytically known task and reward models.

Nevertheless, many recent publications on applications of policy gradient methods in robotics overlooked the newest developments in policy gradient theory and its original roots in the literature. Thus, a large number of heuristic applications of policy gradients can be found, where the success of the projects mainly relied on ingenious initializations and manual parameter tuning of algorithms. A closer inspection often reveals that the chosen methods might be highly biased, or even generate infeasible policies under less fortunate parameter settings, which could lead to unsafe operation of a robot. The main goal of this book chapter is to review which policy gradient methods are applicable to robotics and which issues matter, while also introducing some new policy gradient learning algorithms that seem to have superior performance over previously suggested methods. The remainder of this book chapter will proceed as follows: firstly, we will introduce the general assumptions of reinforcement learning, discuss motor primitives in this framework and pose the problem statement of this book chapter. Secondly, we will discuss the different approaches to policy gradient estimation and discuss their applicability to reinforcement learning of motor primitives. We focus on the most useful methods and discuss several algorithms in-depth. The presented algorithms in this book chapter are highly optimized versions of both novel and previous policy gradient algorithms. Thirdly, we show how these methods can be applied to motor skill learning in robotics and show learning results with a seven degrees of freedom, anthropomorphic SARCOS Master Arm.

---

also been applied in control (Atkeson, 1994; Morimoto & Atkeson, 2003). In this book chapter, we limit ourselves to model-free approaches in order to avoid having to treat model-related approaches.

4.1.1 General Assumptions and Problem Statement

Most robotics domains require the state space and the action spaces to be continuous and high-dimensional such that learning methods based on discretizations are not applicable for higher dimensional systems. However, as the policy is usually implemented on a digital computer, we assume that we can model the control system in a discrete-time manner and we will denote the current time step by k. In order to take possible stochasticity of the plant into account, we denote it using a probability distribution

$$\mathbf{x}_{k+1} \sim p\left(\mathbf{x}_{k+1} \left| \mathbf{x}_k, \mathbf{u}_k\right.\right) \tag{4.1}$$

as model where $\mathbf{u}_k \in \mathbb{R}^M$ denotes the current action, and $\mathbf{x}_k$, $\mathbf{x}_{k+1} \in \mathbb{R}^N$ denote the current and next state, respectively. We furthermore assume that actions are generated by a policy

$$\mathbf{u}_k \sim \pi_{\boldsymbol{\theta}}\left(\mathbf{u}_k \left| \mathbf{x}_k\right.\right) \tag{4.2}$$

which is modeled as a probability distribution in order to incorporate exploratory actions; for some special problems, the optimal solution to a control problem is actually a stochastic controller, see e.g., (Sutton, McAllester, Singh, & Mansour, 2000). The policy is parameterized by some policy parameters $\boldsymbol{\theta} \in \mathbb{R}^K$ and assumed to be continuously differentiable with respect to its parameters $\boldsymbol{\theta}$. The sequence of states and actions forms a trajectory (also called history or roll-out) denoted by $\boldsymbol{\tau} = [\mathbf{x}_{0:H}, \mathbf{u}_{0:H}]$ where H denotes the horizon which can be infinite. At each instant of time, the learning system receives a reward denoted by $r\left(\mathbf{x}_k, \mathbf{u}_k\right) \in \mathbb{R}$.

The general goal of policy optimization in reinforcement learning is to optimize the policy parameters $\boldsymbol{\theta} \in \mathbb{R}^K$ so that the expected return

$$J(\boldsymbol{\theta}) = \frac{1}{a_\Sigma} E\left\{\sum\nolimits_{k=0}^{H} a_k r_k\right\} \tag{4.3}$$

is optimized where a_k denote time-step dependent weighting factors and a_Σ is a normalization factor in order to make sure the weights sum up to one. We require that the weighting factors fulfill $a_{i+j} = a_i a_j$ in order to be able to connect to the previous policy gradient literature; examples are the weights $a_k = \gamma^k$ for discounted reinforcement learning (where γ is in $[0, 1]$) where $a_\Sigma = 1/(1-\gamma)$; alternatively, they are set to $a_k = 1$ for the average reward case where $a_\Sigma = H$. In these cases, we can rewrite the *a normalized expected return* in the form

$$J(\boldsymbol{\theta}) = \int_{\mathbb{X}} d^\pi(\mathbf{x}) \int_{\mathbb{U}} \pi(\mathbf{u}|\mathbf{x}) r(\mathbf{x}, \mathbf{u}) d\mathbf{x} d\mathbf{u} \tag{4.4}$$

used by Sutton et al. (2000), where $d^{\pi}(\mathbf{x}) = a_{\Sigma}^{-1}\sum_{k=0}^{\infty} a_k p(\mathbf{x}_k = \mathbf{x})$ is the weighted state distribution[2].

In general, we assume that for each considered policy $\pi_{\boldsymbol{\theta}}$, a state value function $V^{\pi}(\mathbf{x}, k)$, and the state-action value function $Q^{\pi}(\mathbf{x}, \mathbf{u}, k)$ exist[3] and are given by

$$V^{\pi}(\mathbf{x}, k) = E\left\{\sum\nolimits_{i=k}^{H} a_i r_i \middle| \mathbf{x}_k = \mathbf{x}\right\}, \tag{4.5}$$

$$Q^{\pi}(\mathbf{x}, \mathbf{u}, k) = E\left\{\sum\nolimits_{i=k}^{H} a_i r_i \middle| \mathbf{x}_k = \mathbf{x}, \mathbf{u}_k = \mathbf{u}\right\}. \tag{4.6}$$

In the infinite horizon case, i.e., for $H \to \infty$, we write $V^{\pi}(\mathbf{x})$ and $Q^{\pi}(\mathbf{x}, \mathbf{u})$ as these functions have become time-invariant. Note, that we can define the expected return in terms of the state value function by

$$J(\boldsymbol{\theta}) = \int_{\mathbb{X}} p(\mathbf{x}_0)\, V^{\pi}(\mathbf{x}_0, 0) d\mathbf{x}_0, \tag{4.7}$$

where $p(\mathbf{x}_0)$ is the probability of $\mathbf{x}_0$ being the start-state. Whenever we make practical use of the value function, we assume that we are given good basis functions $\boldsymbol{\phi}(\mathbf{x})$ so that the state-value function can be approximated with linear function approximation $V^{\pi}(\mathbf{x}) = \boldsymbol{\phi}(\mathbf{x})^T \mathbf{v}$.

4.1.2 Motor Primitive Policies

In this section, we first discuss how motor plans can be represented and then how we can bring these into the standard reinforcement learning framework. For this purpose, we consider two forms of motor plans, i.e., (1) *spline-based trajectory plans* and (2) *nonlinear dynamic motor primitives* introduced in (Ijspeert et al., 2002). Spline-based trajectory planning is well-known in the robotics literature, see e.g., (Sciavicco & Siciliano, 2007; Miyamoto et al., 1996). A desired trajectory is represented by piecewise connected polynomials, e.g., we have

$$y_i(t) = \theta_{0i} + \theta_{1i} t + \theta_{2i} t^2 + \theta_{3i} t^3 \tag{4.8}$$

in $t \in [t_i, t_{i+1}]$ under the constraints that both

$$y_i(t_{i+1}) = y_{i+1}(t_{i+1}) \text{ and } \dot{y}_i(t_{i+1}) = \dot{y}_{i+1}(t_{i+1}). \tag{4.9}$$

A given tracking controller, e.g., a PD control law or an inverse dynamics controller, ensures that the trajectory is tracked well. For nonlinear dynamic motor primitives, we use the approach developed in (Ijspeert et al., 2002) where movement plans $(\mathbf{q}_d, \dot{\mathbf{q}}_d)$ for

[2]In most cases, e.g., for $a_k = \gamma^k$, this distribution is a multi-modal mixture distribution even if the distribution $p(x_k = x)$ is a unimodal. Only for $a_k = 1$, the state weighted distribution $d^{\pi}(x)$ will converge to the stationary distribution.

[3]Note that learning in cases where such functions do not exist is usually prohibitively difficult.

each degree of freedom (DOF) of the robot are represented in terms of the time evolution of the nonlinear dynamical systems

$$\ddot{q}_{d,k} = h(q_{d,k}, \mathbf{z}_k, g_k, \tau, \theta_k) \tag{4.10}$$

where $(q_{d,k}, \dot{q}_{d,k})$ denote the desired position and velocity of a joint, z_k the internal state of the dynamic system, g_k the goal (or point attractor) state of each DOF, τ the movement duration shared by all DOFs, and θ_k the open parameters of the function h. The equations used in order to create Equation (4.10) are given in Appendix A.5. The original work in (Ijspeert et al., 2002) demonstrated how the parameters θ_k can be learned to match a template trajectory by means of supervised learning – this scenario is, for instance, useful as the first step of an imitation learning system. Here, we will add the ability of self-improvement of the movement primitives in Equation (4.10) by means of reinforcement learning, which is the crucial second step in imitation learning. The system in Equation (4.10) is a point-to-point movement, i.e., this task is rather well suited for the introduced episodic reinforcement learning methods.

In order to make the reinforcement framework feasible for learning motor primitives, we need to add exploration to the respective motor primitive framework, i.e., we need to add a small perturbation $\epsilon_{d,k} \sim \mathcal{N}(0, \sigma^2)$ so that the nominal target output $\ddot{q}_{d,k}$ becomes the perturbed target output $\ddot{\hat{q}}_{d,k} = \ddot{q}_{d,k} + \epsilon_{d,k}$. By doing so, we obtain a stochastic policy

$$\pi(\ddot{\hat{q}}_{d,k}|q_{d,k}, \mathbf{z}_k, g_k, \tau, \theta_k) = \frac{1}{\sqrt{2\pi\sigma^2}} \exp\left(-\frac{(\ddot{\hat{q}}_{d,k} - \ddot{q}_{d,k})^2}{2\sigma^2}\right). \tag{4.11}$$

This policy will be used throughout the book chapter. It is particularly practical as the exploration can be easily controlled through only one variable σ.

4.2 Policy Gradient Approaches for Parameterized Motor Primitives

The general goal of policy optimization in reinforcement learning is to optimize the policy parameters $\boldsymbol{\theta} \in R^K$ so that the expected return $J(\boldsymbol{\theta})$ is maximal. For motor primitive

Table 4.1: General setup for policy gradient reinforcement learning.

input: initial policy parameterization $\boldsymbol{\theta}_0$.	
1	**repeat**
2	obtain policy gradient g from estimator (see Tables 4.2-4.7)
3	update policy $\boldsymbol{\theta}_{h+1} = \boldsymbol{\theta}_h + \alpha_h \mathbf{g}$.
4	**until** policy parameterization $\boldsymbol{\theta}_h \approx \boldsymbol{\theta}_{h+1}$ converges
return: optimal policy parameters $\boldsymbol{\theta}^* = \boldsymbol{\theta}_{h+1}$.	

learning in robotics, we require that any change to the policy parameterization has to be smooth as drastic changes can be hazardous for the robot and its environnment. Also, it would render initializations of the policy based on domain knowledge or imitation learning useless, as these would otherwise vanish after a single update step. Additionally, we need to guarantee that the policy is improved in the update steps at least on average which rules out greedy value function based methods. For these reasons, policy gradient methods which follow the steepest descent on the expected return are the method of choice. These methods update the policy parameterization according to the gradient update rule

$$\boldsymbol{\theta}_{h+1} = \boldsymbol{\theta}_h + \alpha_h \left. \nabla_{\boldsymbol{\theta}} J \right|_{\boldsymbol{\theta}=\boldsymbol{\theta}_h}, \tag{4.12}$$

where $\alpha_h \in \mathbb{R}^+$ denotes a learning rate. If the gradient estimate is unbiased and learning rates fulfill

$$\sum_{h=0}^{\infty} \alpha_h > 0 \text{ and} \sum_{h=0}^{\infty} \alpha_h^2 = 0, \tag{4.13}$$

the learning process is guaranteed to converge to at least a local minimum.

The main problem in policy gradient methods is to obtain a good estimator of the policy gradient $\left. \nabla_{\boldsymbol{\theta}} J \right|_{\boldsymbol{\theta}=\boldsymbol{\theta}_h}$. Traditionally, people have used deterministic model-based methods for obtaining the gradient (Jacobson & Mayne, 1970; Dyer & McReynolds, 1970; Hasdorff, 1976). However, in order to become autonomous we cannot expect to be able to model every detail of the robot and environment appropriately. Therefore, we need to estimate the policy gradient only from data generated during the execution of a task, i.e., without the need for a model. In this section, we will study different approaches and discuss which of these are useful in robotics.

The literature on policy gradient methods has yielded a variety of estimation methods over the last years. The most prominent approaches, which have been applied to robotics are finite-difference and likelihood ratio methods, more well-known as REINFORCE methods in reinforcement learning.

4.2.1 Finite-difference Methods

Finite-difference methods are among the oldest policy gradient approaches dating back to the 1950s; they originated from the stochastic simulation community and are quite straightforward to understand. The policy parameterization is varied by small increments $\Delta\boldsymbol{\theta}_i$ and for each policy parameter variation $\boldsymbol{\theta}_h + \Delta\boldsymbol{\theta}_i$ roll-outs are performed which generate estimates $\Delta\hat{J}_j \approx J(\boldsymbol{\theta}_h + \Delta\boldsymbol{\theta}_i) - J_{\text{ref}}$ of the expected return. There are different ways of choosing the reference value J_{ref}, e.g. forward-difference estimators with $J_{\text{ref}} = J(\boldsymbol{\theta}_h)$ and central-difference estimators with $J_{\text{ref}} = J(\boldsymbol{\theta}_h - \Delta\boldsymbol{\theta}_i)$. The most general way is to formulate the determination of the reference value J_{ref} and the policy gradient estimate $\mathbf{g}_{\text{FD}} \approx \left. \nabla_{\boldsymbol{\theta}} J \right|_{\boldsymbol{\theta}=\boldsymbol{\theta}_h}$ as a regression problem which can be solved by

$$\left[\mathbf{g}_{\text{FD}}^T, J_{\text{ref}}\right]^T = \left(\Delta\Theta^T \Delta\Theta\right)^{-1} \Delta\Theta^T \hat{\mathbf{J}}, \tag{4.14}$$

Table 4.2: Finite difference gradient estimator.

input: policy parameterization $\boldsymbol{\theta}$.	
1	**repeat**
2	generate policy variation $\Delta\boldsymbol{\theta}_i$.
3	estimate $J(\boldsymbol{\theta}+\Delta\boldsymbol{\theta}_i) \approx \hat{J}_j = \sum_{k=0}^{H} a_k r_k$ from rollouts.
4	compute gradient $\left[\mathbf{g}_{\mathrm{FD}}^T, J_{\mathrm{ref}}\right]^T = \left(\Delta\Theta^T\Delta\Theta\right)^{-1}\Delta\Theta^T\hat{\mathbf{J}}$. with $\Delta\Theta^T = \begin{bmatrix}\Delta\boldsymbol{\theta}_1, & \ldots, & \Delta\boldsymbol{\theta}_I \\ 1, & \ldots, & 1\end{bmatrix}$, and $\hat{\mathbf{J}}^T = [\hat{J}_1, \ldots, \hat{J}_I]$.
5	**until** gradient estimate $\mathbf{g}_{\mathrm{FD}}$ converged.
return: gradient estimate $\mathbf{g}_{\mathrm{FD}}$.	

where

$$\Delta\Theta = \begin{bmatrix}\Delta\boldsymbol{\theta}_1, & \ldots, & \Delta\boldsymbol{\theta}_I \\ 1, & \ldots, & 1\end{bmatrix}^T, \text{ and} \tag{4.15}$$

$$\hat{\mathbf{J}} = [\hat{J}_1, \ldots, \hat{J}_I]^T, \tag{4.16}$$

denote the I samples. If single parameters are perturbed, this method is known as the Kiefer-Wolfowitz procedure and if multiple parameters are perturbed simultaneously, it is known as Simultaneous Perturbation Stochastic gradient Approximation (SPSA), see (Sadegh & Spall, 1997; Spall, 2003) for in-depth treatment. This approach can been highly efficient in simulation optimization of deterministic systems (Spall, 2003) or when a common history of random numbers (Glynn, 1987; Kleinman, Spall, & Naiman, 1999) is being used (the later trick is known as the PEGASUS method in reinforcement learning, see (Ng & Jordan, 2000)), and can get close to a convergence rate of $O(I^{-1/2})$ (Glynn, 1987). However, when used on a real system, the uncertainities degrade the performance resulting in convergence rates ranging between $O(I^{-1/4})$ to $O(I^{-2/5})$ depending on the chosen reference value (Glynn, 1987). An implementation of this algorithm is shown in Table 4.2.

Due to the simplicity of this approach, such methods have been successfully applied to robot motor skill learning in numerous applications (Miyamoto et al., 1995, 1996; Tedrake et al., 2005; Kohl & Stone, 2004; Mitsunaga et al., 2005). However, the straightforward application is not without peril as the generation of the $\Delta\boldsymbol{\theta}_j$ requires proper knowledge on the system, as badly chosen $\Delta\boldsymbol{\theta}_j$ can destabilize the policy so that the system becomes instable and the gradient estimation process is prone to fail. Even in the field of simulation optimization where the destabilization of the system is not such a dangerous issue, the careful generation of the parameter perturbation is a topic of debate with strong requirements on the generating process (Sadegh & Spall, 1997). Practical

Table 4.3: General likelihood ratio policy gradient estimator "Episodic REINFORCE" with an optimal baseline.

input: policy parameterization $\boldsymbol{\theta}$.

repeat
  perform a trial and obtain $\mathbf{x}_{0:H}, \mathbf{u}_{0:H}, r_{0:H}$
  for each gradient element g_h
    estimate optimal baseline
    $$b^h = \frac{\left\langle \left(\sum_{k=0}^{H} \nabla_{\theta_h} \log \pi_{\boldsymbol{\theta}}(\mathbf{u}_k|\mathbf{x}_k) \right)^2 \sum_{l=0}^{H} a_l r_l \right\rangle}{\left\langle \left(\sum_{k=0}^{H} \nabla_{\theta_h} \log \pi_{\boldsymbol{\theta}}(\mathbf{u}_k|\mathbf{x}_k) \right)^2 \right\rangle}$$
    estimate the gradient element
    $$g_h = \left\langle \left(\sum_{k=0}^{H} \nabla_{\theta_h} \log \pi_{\boldsymbol{\theta}}(\mathbf{u}_k|\mathbf{x}_k) \right) \left(\sum_{l=0}^{H} a_l r_l - b^h \right) \right\rangle .$$
  end for.
until gradient estimate $\mathbf{g}_{\text{RF}}$ converged.

return: gradient estimate $\mathbf{g}_{\text{RF}}$.

problems often require that each element of the vector $\Delta\boldsymbol{\theta}_j$ has a different order of magnitude, making the generation particularly difficult. Therefore, this approach can only applied under strict human supervision.

4.2.2 Likelihood Ratio Methods and REINFORCE

Likelihood ratio methods are driven by an important different insight. Assume that trajectories $\boldsymbol{\tau}$ are generated from a system by roll-outs, i.e., $\boldsymbol{\tau} \sim p_{\boldsymbol{\theta}}(\boldsymbol{\tau}) = p(\boldsymbol{\tau}|\,\boldsymbol{\theta})$ with rewards $r(\boldsymbol{\tau}) = \sum_{k=0}^{H} a_k r_k$. In this case, the policy gradient can be estimated using the likelihood ratio trick, see e.g. (Aleksandrov, Sysoyev, & Shemeneva, 1968; Glynn, 1987), or REINFORCE trick (Williams, 1992), i.e., we can rewrite the gradient by

$$\begin{aligned} \nabla_{\boldsymbol{\theta}} J(\boldsymbol{\theta}) &= \int_{\mathbb{T}} \nabla_{\boldsymbol{\theta}} p_{\boldsymbol{\theta}}(\boldsymbol{\tau})\, r(\boldsymbol{\tau}) d\boldsymbol{\tau} = \int_{\mathbb{T}} p_{\boldsymbol{\theta}}(\boldsymbol{\tau})\, \nabla_{\boldsymbol{\theta}} \log p_{\boldsymbol{\theta}}(\boldsymbol{\tau})\, r(\boldsymbol{\tau}) d\boldsymbol{\tau}, \\ &= E\left\{ \nabla_{\boldsymbol{\theta}} \log p_{\boldsymbol{\theta}}(\boldsymbol{\tau})\, r(\boldsymbol{\tau}) \right\}. \end{aligned} \tag{4.17}$$

Importantly, the derivative $\nabla_{\boldsymbol{\theta}} \log p_{\boldsymbol{\theta}}(\boldsymbol{\tau})$ can be computed without knowleged of the generating distribution $p_{\boldsymbol{\theta}}(\boldsymbol{\tau})$ as

$$p_{\boldsymbol{\theta}}(\boldsymbol{\tau}) = p(\mathbf{x}_0) \prod_{k=0}^{H} p(\mathbf{x}_{k+1}|\mathbf{x}_k, \mathbf{u}_k)\, \pi_{\boldsymbol{\theta}}(\mathbf{u}_k|\mathbf{x}_k) \tag{4.18}$$

implies that

$$\nabla_{\boldsymbol{\theta}} \log p_{\boldsymbol{\theta}}(\boldsymbol{\tau}) = \sum_{k=0}^{H} \nabla_{\boldsymbol{\theta}} \log \pi_{\boldsymbol{\theta}}(\mathbf{u}_k|\mathbf{x}_k), \tag{4.19}$$

i.e., the derivatives through the control system do not have to be computed[4]. As

$$\int_{\mathbb{T}} p_{\boldsymbol{\theta}}\left(\boldsymbol{\tau}\right) \nabla_{\boldsymbol{\theta}} \log p_{\boldsymbol{\theta}}\left(\boldsymbol{\tau}\right) d\boldsymbol{\tau} = \int_{\mathbb{T}} \nabla_{\boldsymbol{\theta}} p_{\boldsymbol{\theta}}\left(\boldsymbol{\tau}\right) d\boldsymbol{\tau} = \nabla_{\boldsymbol{\theta}} 1 = 0, \tag{4.20}$$

a constant baseline can be inserted resulting into the gradient estimator

$$\nabla_{\boldsymbol{\theta}} J\left(\boldsymbol{\theta}\right) = E\left\{\nabla_{\boldsymbol{\theta}} \log p_{\boldsymbol{\theta}}\left(\boldsymbol{\tau}\right)\left(r(\boldsymbol{\tau}) - b\right)\right\}, \tag{4.21}$$

where $b \in \mathbb{R}$ can be chosen arbitrarily (Williams, 1992) but usually with the goal to minimize the variance of the gradient estimator. Note that the baseline was most likely first suggested by Williams (1992) and is unique to reinforcement learning as it requires a separation of the policy from the state-transition probability densities. Therefore, the general path likelihood ratio estimator or episodic REINFORCE gradient estimator (Williams, 1992) is given by

$$\mathbf{g}_{\mathrm{RF}} = \left\langle \left(\sum\nolimits_{k=0}^{H} \nabla_{\boldsymbol{\theta}} \log \pi_{\boldsymbol{\theta}}\left(\mathbf{u}_k \left| \mathbf{x}_k \right.\right)\right) \left(\sum\nolimits_{l=0}^{H} a_l r_l - b\right) \right\rangle, \tag{4.22}$$

where $\langle f\left(\boldsymbol{\tau}\right)\rangle = \int_{\mathbb{T}} f(\boldsymbol{\tau})\, d\boldsymbol{\tau}$ denotes the average over trajectories. This type of method is guaranteed to converge to the true gradient at the fastest theoretically possible pace of $O(I^{-1/2})$ where I denotes the number of roll-outs (Glynn, 1987) even if the data is generated from a highly stochastic system. An implementation of this algorithm will be shown in Table 4.3 together with the estimator for the optimal baseline.

Besides the theoretically faster convergence rate, likelihood ratio gradient methods have a variety of advantages in comparison to finite difference methods. As the generation of policy parameter variations is no longer needed, the complicated control of these variables can no longer endanger the gradient estimation process. Furthermore, in practice, already a single roll-out can suffice for an unbiased gradient estimate (Baxter & Bartlett, 2001; Spall, 2003) viable for a good policy update step, thus reducing the amount of roll-outs needed. Finally, this approach has yielded the most real-world robot motor learning results (Nakamura et al., 2004; Mori et al., 2004; Endo et al., 2005; Benbrahim & Franklin, 1997; Kimura & Kobayashi, 1997; Peters et al., 2005; Gullapalli et al., 1994). In the subsequent two sections, we will strive to explain and improve this type of gradient estimator.

[4]This result makes an important difference: in stochastic system optimization, finite difference estimators are often prefered as the derivative through system is required but not known. In policy search, we always know the derivative of the policy with respect to its parameters and therefore we can make use of the theoretical advantages of likelihood ratio gradient estimators.

4.3 'Vanilla' Policy Gradient Approaches

Despite the fast asymptotic convergence speed of the gradient estimate, the variance of the likelihood-ratio gradient estimator can be problematic in theory as well as in practice. This can be illustrated straightforwardly with an example.

Example 4.1 *When using a REINFORCE estimator with a baseline $b = 0$ in a scenario where there is only a single reward of always the same magnitude, e.g., $r(\mathbf{x}, \mathbf{u}) = c \in R$ for all $\mathbf{x}, \mathbf{u}$, then the variance of the gradient estimate will grow at least cubically with the length of the planning horizon H as*

$$\mathrm{Var}\{g_{RF}\} = H^2 c^2 \sum\nolimits_{k=0}^{H} \mathrm{Var}\{\nabla_{\boldsymbol{\theta}} \log \pi_{\boldsymbol{\theta}} (\mathbf{u}_k | \mathbf{x}_k)\}, \tag{4.23}$$

if $\mathrm{Var}\{\nabla_{\boldsymbol{\theta}} \log \pi_{\boldsymbol{\theta}} (\mathbf{u}_k | \mathbf{x}_k)\} > 0$ *for all k. Furthemore, it will also grow quadratically with the magnitude of the reward c.*

For this reason, we need to address this issue and we will discuss several advances in likelihood ratio policy gradient optimization, i.e., the policy gradient theorem/GPOMDP, optimal baselines and the compatible function approximation.

4.3.1 Policy gradient theorem and G(PO)MDP

The trivial observation that future actions do not depend on past rewards (unless policy changes take place continuously during the trajectory) can result in a significant reduction of the variance of the policy gradient estimate. This insight can be formalized as

$$E\{\nabla_{\boldsymbol{\theta}} \log \pi_{\boldsymbol{\theta}} (\mathbf{u}_l | \mathbf{x}_l) r_k\} = E\{\underbrace{E\{\nabla_{\boldsymbol{\theta}} \log \pi_{\boldsymbol{\theta}} (\mathbf{u}_l | \mathbf{x}_l) | x_k\}}_{=0} r_k\} = 0 \tag{4.24}$$

for $l > k$, which is straightforward to verify. This allows two variations of the previous algorithm which are known as the policy gradient theorem (Sutton et al., 2000)

$$\mathbf{g}_{\text{PGT}} = \left\langle \sum\nolimits_{k=0}^{H} a_k \nabla_{\boldsymbol{\theta}} \log \pi_{\boldsymbol{\theta}} (\mathbf{u}_k | \mathbf{x}_k) \left(\sum\nolimits_{l=k}^{H} a_{l-k} r_l - b_k \right) \right\rangle, \tag{4.25}$$

or G(PO)MD (Baxter & Bartlett, 2001)

$$\mathbf{g}_{\text{GMDP}} = \left\langle \sum\nolimits_{l=0}^{H} \left(\sum\nolimits_{k=0}^{l} \nabla_{\boldsymbol{\theta}} \log \pi_{\boldsymbol{\theta}} (\mathbf{u}_k | \mathbf{x}_k) \right) (a_l r_l - b_l) \right\rangle, \tag{4.26}$$

While these algorithms *look* different, they are *exactly equivalent* in their gradient estimate[5], i.e.,

$$\mathbf{g}_{\text{PGT}} = \mathbf{g}_{\text{GMPD}}, \tag{4.27}$$

which is a direct result from the summation theorem (Vachenauer, Rade, & Westergren, 2000) and from the fact that they can both derived from REINFORCE. The G(PO)MDP formulation has previously been derived in the simulation optimization community (Glynn, 1990). An implementation of this algorithm is shown together with the optimal baseline in Table 4.4.

These two forms originally puzzled the community as they were derived from two separate points of view (Sutton et al., 2000; Baxter & Bartlett, 2001) and seemed to be different on first inspection. While their equality is natural when taking the path-based perspective, we will obtain the forms proposed in the original sources in a few steps. First, let us note that in Equation (4.25) the term $\sum_{l=k}^{\infty} a_l r_l$ in the policy gradient theorem is equivalent to a monte-carlo estimate of the value function $Q^{\pi}(\mathbf{x}, \mathbf{u})$. Thus, we obtain

$$\mathbf{g}_{\text{PGT}} = \int_{\mathbb{X}} d^{\pi}(\mathbf{x}) \int_{\mathbb{U}} \nabla_{\boldsymbol{\theta}} \pi_{\boldsymbol{\theta}}(\mathbf{u}|\mathbf{x}) \left(Q^{\pi}(\mathbf{x}, \mathbf{u}) - b(x)\right) d\mathbf{u} d\mathbf{x}, \tag{4.28}$$

for normalized weightings with infinite horizons (e.g., using the discounted or the average reward case) and while employing the value function instead of the sum. This form has a significant advantage over REINFORCE-like expressions, i.e., it is obvious that the variance does not grow with the planning horizon if a good estimate of $Q^{\pi}(\mathbf{x}, \mathbf{u})$ is given, e.g., using traditional value function methods. Thus, the counterexample from Example 4.1 does no longer apply. Similarly, the term $\sum_{k=0}^{l} \nabla_{\boldsymbol{\theta}} \log \pi_{\boldsymbol{\theta}}(\mathbf{u}_k|\mathbf{x}_k)$ becomes the log-derivative of the distribution of states $\mu_k^{\pi}(\mathbf{x}) = p(\mathbf{x} = x_k)$ at step k in expectation, i.e.,

$$\nabla_{\boldsymbol{\theta}} \log d^{\pi}(\mathbf{x}) = \sum_{l=0}^{H} a_l \nabla_{\boldsymbol{\theta}} \log \mu_k^{\pi}(\mathbf{x}) = \sum_{l=0}^{H} a_l \sum_{k=0}^{l} \nabla_{\boldsymbol{\theta}} \log \pi_{\boldsymbol{\theta}}(\mathbf{u}_k|\mathbf{x}_k), \tag{4.29}$$

which then can be used to rewrite the G(PO)MDP estimator into state-space form, i.e.,

$$\mathbf{g}_{\text{GMDP}} = \int_{\mathbb{X}} \int_{\mathbb{U}} \left(\pi_{\boldsymbol{\theta}}(\mathbf{u}|\mathbf{x}) \nabla_{\boldsymbol{\theta}} d^{\pi}(\mathbf{x}) + d^{\pi}(\mathbf{x}) \nabla_{\boldsymbol{\theta}} \pi_{\boldsymbol{\theta}}(\mathbf{u}|\mathbf{x})\right) \left(r(\mathbf{x}, \mathbf{u}) - b\right) d\mathbf{u} d\mathbf{x}. \tag{4.30}$$

Note that this form only allows a baseline which is independent of the state unlike the policy gradient theorem. When either of the state-action value function or the state distribution derivative can be easily obtained by derivation or estimation, the variance of the gradient can be reduced significantly.Without a formal derivation of it, the policy gradient theorem has been applied in (Gullapalli, 1991; Kimura & Kobayashi, 1997) using estimated value functions $Q^{\pi}(\mathbf{x}, \mathbf{u})$ instead of the term $\sum_{l=k}^{H} a_l r_l$ and a baseline

[5]Note that (Baxter & Bartlett, 2001) additionally add an eligibility trick for reweighting trajectory pieces. This trick can be highly dangerous in robotics; it can be demonstrated that even in linear-quadratic regulation, this trick can result in convergence to the worst possible policies for small planning horizons (i.e., small eligibility rates).

Table 4.4: Specialized likelihood ratio policy gradient estimator "G(PO)MDP"/Policy Gradient with an optimal baseline.

input: policy parameterization $\boldsymbol{\theta}$.

repeat
  perform trials and obtain $\mathbf{x}_{0:H}, \mathbf{u}_{0:H}, r_{0:H}$
  for each gradient element g_h
    for each time step k
      estimate baseline for time step k by
      $b_k^h = \frac{\left\langle \left(\sum_{\kappa=0}^{k} \nabla_{\theta_h} \log \pi_{\boldsymbol{\theta}}(\mathbf{u}_\kappa | \mathbf{x}_\kappa) \right)^2 a_k r_k \right\rangle}{\left\langle \left(\sum_{\kappa=0}^{k} \nabla_{\theta_h} \log \pi_{\boldsymbol{\theta}}(\mathbf{u}_\kappa | \mathbf{x}_\kappa) \right)^2 \right\rangle}$
    end for.
    estimate the gradient element
    $g_h = \left\langle \sum_{l=0}^{H} \left(\sum_{k=0}^{l} \nabla_{\theta_h} \log \pi_{\boldsymbol{\theta}} (\mathbf{u}_k | \mathbf{x}_k) \right) (a_l r_l - b_l^h) \right\rangle.$
  end for.
until gradient estimate $\mathbf{g}_{\mathrm{GMDP}}$ converged.

return: gradient estimate $\mathbf{g}_{\mathrm{GMDP}}$.

$b_k = V^\pi(\mathbf{x}_k, k)$. Note that the version introduced in (Kimura & Kobayashi, 1997) is biased[6] and does not correspond to the correct gradient unlike (Gullapalli, 1991).

Note that the formulation over paths can be used in a more general fashion than the state-action form, e.g., it allows derivations for non-stationary policies, rewards and systems, than the state-action formulation in the paragraph above. However, for some results, it is more convenient to use the state-action based formulation and there we will make use of it.

4.3.2 Optimal Baselines

Above, we have already introduced the concept of a baseline which can decrease the variance of a policy gradient estimate by orders of magnitude. Thus, an optimal selection of such a baseline is essential. An optimal baseline minimizes the variance $\sigma_h^2 = \mathrm{Var}\{g_h\}$ of each element g_h of the gradient $\mathbf{g}$ *without* biasing the gradient estimate, i.e., violating $E\{\mathbf{g}\} = \nabla_{\boldsymbol{\theta}} J$. This can be phrased as having a seperate baseline b^h for every element of the gradient[7], i.e., we have

$$\min_{b_h} \sigma_h^2 = \mathrm{Var}\{g_h\}, \tag{4.31}$$

[6] See Appendix A.3 for more information.

[7] A single baseline for all parameters can also be obtained and is more common in the reinforcement learning literature (Weaver & Tao, 2001a; Greensmith, Bartlett, & Baxter, 2004; Weaver & Tao, 2001b; Williams, 1992; Lawrence, Cowan, & Russell, 2003; Greensmith, Bartlett, & Baxter, 2001). However, such a baseline is of course suboptimal.

$$s.t. E\{g_h\} = \nabla_{\theta_h} J. \tag{4.32}$$

Due to the requirement of unbiasedness of the gradient estimate, we have $\sigma_h^2 = E\{g_h^2\} - (\nabla_{\theta_h} J)^2$, and due to

$$\min_{b_h} \sigma_h^2 \geq E\left\{\min_{b_h} g_h^2\right\} - (\nabla_{\theta_h} J)^2, \tag{4.33}$$

the optimal baseline for each gradient element g_h can always be given by

$$b^h = \frac{\left\langle \left(\sum_{k=0}^{H} \nabla_{\theta_h} \log \pi_{\boldsymbol{\theta}} \left(\mathbf{u}_k \left|\mathbf{x}_k\right.\right)\right)^2 \sum_{l=0}^{H} a_l r_l \right\rangle}{\left\langle \left(\sum_{k=0}^{H} \nabla_{\theta_h} \log \pi_{\boldsymbol{\theta}} \left(\mathbf{u}_k \left|\mathbf{x}_k\right.\right)\right)^2 \right\rangle} \tag{4.34}$$

for the general likelihood ratio gradient estimator, i.e., Episodic REINFORCE. The algorithmic form of the optimal baseline is shown in Table 4.3 in line 4. If the sums in the baselines are modified appropriately, we can obtain the optimal baseline for the policy gradient theorem or G(PO)MPD. We only show G(PO)MDP in this book chapter in Table 4.4 as the policy gradient theorem is numerically equivalent.

The optimal baseline which does not bias the gradient in Episodic REINFORCE can only be a single number for all trajectories and in G(PO)MPD it can also depend on the time-step (Peters, 2005). However, in the policy gradient theorem it can depend on the current state and, therefore, if a good parameterization for the baseline is known, e.g., in a generalized linear form $b(\mathbf{x}_k) = \phi(\mathbf{x}_k)^T \omega$, this can significantly improve the gradient estimation process. However, the selection of the basis functions $\phi(\mathbf{x}_k)$ can be difficult and often impractical in practice. See (Weaver & Tao, 2001a; Greensmith et al., 2004; Weaver & Tao, 2001b; Williams, 1992; Lawrence et al., 2003; Greensmith et al., 2001) for more information on this topic.

4.3.3 Compatible Function Approximation

As we previously discussed, the largest source of variance in the formulation of Equation (4.28) is the state-action value function $Q^\pi(\mathbf{x}, \mathbf{u})$, especially if the function $Q^\pi(\mathbf{x}, \mathbf{u})$ is approximated by rollouts as in this context. The natural alternative of using approximate value functions is problematic as these introduce bias in presence of imperfect basis function. However, as demonstrated in (Sutton et al., 2000) and (Konda & Tsitsiklis, 2000) the term $Q^\pi(\mathbf{x}, \mathbf{u}) - b^\pi(\mathbf{x})$ can be replaced by a compatible function approximation

$$f_w^\pi(\mathbf{x}, \mathbf{u}) = (\nabla_{\boldsymbol{\theta}} \log \pi(\mathbf{u}|\mathbf{x}))^T \mathbf{w} \equiv Q^\pi(\mathbf{x}, \mathbf{u}) - b^\pi(\mathbf{x}), \tag{4.35}$$

parameterized by the vector $\mathbf{w}$, *without* affecting the unbiasedness of the gradient estimate and irrespective of the choice of the baseline $b^\pi(\mathbf{x})$. However, as mentioned in (Sutton et al., 2000), the baseline may still be useful in order to reduce the variance of the gradient estimate when Equation (4.28) is approximated from samples. Based on Equations (4.28, 4.35), we derive an estimate of the policy gradient as

$$\nabla_{\boldsymbol{\theta}} J(\boldsymbol{\theta}) = \int_{\mathbb{X}} d^{\pi}(\mathbf{x}) \int_{\mathbb{U}} \pi(\mathbf{u}|\mathbf{x}) \nabla_{\boldsymbol{\theta}} \log \pi(\mathbf{u}|\mathbf{x}) \nabla_{\boldsymbol{\theta}} \log \pi(\mathbf{u}|\mathbf{x})^{T} d\mathbf{u} d\mathbf{x}\, \mathbf{w} = F_{\boldsymbol{\theta}} \mathbf{w}. \quad (4.36)$$

as $\nabla_{\boldsymbol{\theta}} \pi(\mathbf{u}|\mathbf{x}) = \pi(\mathbf{u}|\mathbf{x}) \nabla_{\boldsymbol{\theta}} \log \pi(\mathbf{u}|\mathbf{x})$. Since $\pi(\mathbf{u}|\mathbf{x})$ is chosen by the user, even in sampled data, the integral $\mathbf{G}(\mathbf{x}) = \int_{\mathbb{U}} \pi(\mathbf{u}|\mathbf{x}) \nabla_{\boldsymbol{\theta}} \log \pi(\mathbf{u}|\mathbf{x}) \nabla_{\boldsymbol{\theta}} \log \pi(\mathbf{u}|\mathbf{x})^{T} d\mathbf{u}$ can be evaluated analytically or empirically without actually executing all actions. It is also noteworthy that the baseline does not appear in Equation (4.36) as it integrates out, thus eliminating the need to find an optimal selection of this open parameter. Nevertheless, the estimation of $\mathbf{G} = \int_{\mathbb{X}} d^{\pi}(\mathbf{x}) \mathbf{G}(\mathbf{x}) d\mathbf{x}$ is still expensive since $d^{\pi}(\mathbf{x})$ ist not known.

An important observation is that the compatible function approximation $f_{\mathbf{w}}^{\pi}(\mathbf{x}, \mathbf{u})$ is mean-zero w.r.t. the action distribution, i.e.,

$$\int_{\mathbb{U}} \pi(\mathbf{u}|\mathbf{x}) f_{\mathbf{w}}^{\pi}(\mathbf{x}, \mathbf{u}) d\mathbf{u} = \mathbf{w}^{T} \int_{\mathbb{U}} \nabla_{\boldsymbol{\theta}} \pi(\mathbf{u}|\mathbf{x}) d\mathbf{u} = 0, \quad (4.37)$$

since from $\int_{\mathbb{U}} \pi(\mathbf{u}|\mathbf{x}) d\mathbf{u} = 1$, differention w.r.t. to θ results in $\int_{\mathbb{U}} \nabla_{\boldsymbol{\theta}} \pi(\mathbf{u}|\mathbf{x}) d\mathbf{u} = 0$. Thus, $f_{w}^{\pi}(\mathbf{x}, \mathbf{u})$ represents an *advantage function* $A^{\pi}(\mathbf{x}, \mathbf{u}) = Q^{\pi}(\mathbf{x}, \mathbf{u}) - V^{\pi}(\mathbf{x})$ in general. The advantage function *cannot* be learned with TD-like bootstrapping without knowledge of the value function as the essence of TD is to compare the value $V^{\pi}(\mathbf{x})$ of the two adjacent states – but this value has been subtracted out in $A^{\pi}(\mathbf{x}, \mathbf{u})$. Hence, a TD-like bootstrapping using exclusively the compatible function approximator is impossible. As an alternative, (Sutton et al., 2000; Konda & Tsitsiklis, 2000) suggested to approximate $f_{w}^{\pi}(\mathbf{x}, \mathbf{u})$ from unbiased estimates $\hat{Q}^{\pi}(\mathbf{x}, \mathbf{u})$ of the action value function, e.g., obtained from roll-outs and using least-squares minimization between f_{w} and $\hat{Q}^{\pi}$. While possible in theory, one needs to realize that this approach implies a function approximation problem where the parameterization of the function approximator only spans a much smaller subspace of the training data – e.g., imagine approximating a quadratic function with a line. In practice, the results of such an approximation depends crucially on the training data distribution and has thus unacceptably high variance – e.g., fit a line to only data from the right branch of a parabula, the left branch, or data from both branches. In the next section, we will see that there are smarter ways to estimate the compatible function approximation (Section 4.4.1) and that this compatible function approximation has a special meaning (Section 4.4.2).

4.4 Natural Actor-Critic

Despite all the advances in the variance reduction of policy gradient methods, these methods tend to perform surprisingly poorly. Even when applied to simple examples with rather few states, where the gradient can be determined very accurately, they turn out to be quite inefficient – thus, the underlying reason cannot be the variance in the gradient estimate but rather be caused by the large plateaus in the expected return landscape where the gradients are small and often do not point directly towards the optimal solution. A simple example that demonstrates this behavior is given in Fig. 4.1. Similar to supervised learning, steepest ascent with respect to the Fisher information metric (Amari, 1998), called the 'natural' policy gradient, turns out to be significantly more efficient than normal gradients. Such an approach was first suggested for reinforcement learning as the 'average natural policy gradient' in (Kakade, 2002), and subsequently shown to be the true natural policy gradient (Peters et al., 2003a; Bagnell & Schneider, 2003). In this book chapter, we take this line of reasoning one step further by introducing the Natural Actor-Critic which inherits the convergence guarantees from gradient methods.

Several properties of the natural policy gradient are worth highlighting:

- Convergence to a local minimum is guaranteed, see (Amari, 1998).
- By choosing a more direct path to the optimal solution in parameter space, the natural gradient has, from empirical observations, faster convergence and avoids premature convergence of 'vanilla gradients' (see Figure 4.1).
- The natural policy gradient can be shown to be **covariant**, i.e., independent of the coordinate frame chosen for expressing the policy parameters (see Section 4.5.1).
- As the natural gradient analytically averages out the influence of the stochastic policy (including the baseline of the function approximator), it requires fewer data points for a good gradient estimate than 'vanilla gradients'.

4.4.1 Motivation

One of the main reasons for using policy gradient methods is that we intend to do just a small change $\Delta\boldsymbol{\theta}$ to the policy $\pi_{\boldsymbol{\theta}}$ while improving the policy. However, the meaning of small is ambiguous. When using the Euclidian metric of $\sqrt{\Delta\boldsymbol{\theta}^T\Delta\boldsymbol{\theta}}$, then the gradient is different for every parameterization $\boldsymbol{\theta}$ of the policy $\pi_{\boldsymbol{\theta}}$ even if these parameterizations are related to each other by a linear transformation (Kakade, 2002), often resulting in unnaturally slow learning even when higher order gradient methods were employed (Baxter, Bartlett, & Weaver, 2001; Berny, 2000; Kakade, 2001). This problem poses the question whether we can achieve a covariant gradient descent, i.e., gradient descent with respect to an invariant measure of the closeness between the current policy and the updated policy based upon the distribution of the paths generated by each of these. In statistics, a variety of distance measures for the closeness of two distributions (e.g., $p_{\boldsymbol{\theta}}(\boldsymbol{\tau})$ and $p_{\boldsymbol{\theta}+\Delta\boldsymbol{\theta}}(\boldsymbol{\tau})$) have been suggested, e.g., the Kullback-Leibler divergence[8] $d_{\mathrm{KL}}(p_{\boldsymbol{\theta}}(\boldsymbol{\tau})\,||p_{\boldsymbol{\theta}+\Delta\boldsymbol{\theta}}(\boldsymbol{\tau}))$, the Hellinger distance d_{HD} and others (Su & Gibbs, 2002). Many of these distances (e.g.,

[8]While being 'the natural way to think about closeness in probability distributions' (Balasubramanian, 1997), this measure is technically not a metric as it is not commutative.

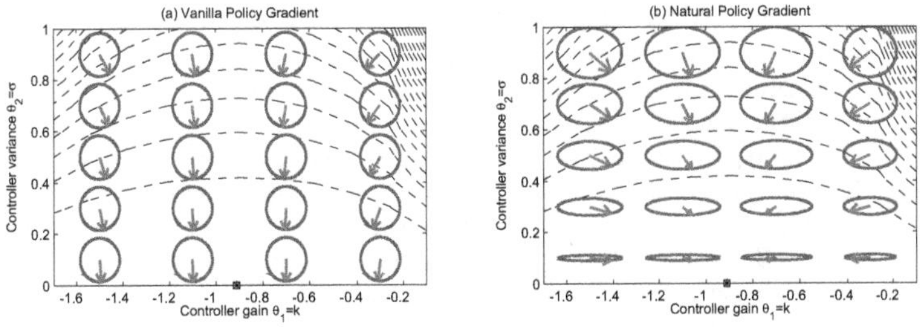

Figure 4.1: The classical example of LQR can be used to illustrate why 'vanilla' policy gradients reduce the exploration to zero while natural policy gradients go for the optimal solution. The blue circle in (a) indicate equal distance with the standard Eucledian metric, while the one in (b) shows equal distance with respect to the Fisher information metric. The natural policy gradient corresponds to searching the steepest descent on an infinitesimally small Fisher ellipse (b), while the vanilla policy gradient corresponds to steepest descent on a unit circle.

the previously mentioned ones) can be approximated by the same second order Taylor expansion, i.e., by

$$d_{\mathrm{KL}}\left(p_{\boldsymbol{\theta}}\left(\boldsymbol{\tau}\right)||p_{\boldsymbol{\theta}+\boldsymbol{\Delta\theta}}\left(\boldsymbol{\tau}\right)\right) \approx \frac{1}{2}\boldsymbol{\Delta\theta}^T\mathbf{F}_{\boldsymbol{\theta}}\,\boldsymbol{\Delta\theta}, \tag{4.38}$$

where

$$\mathbf{F}_{\boldsymbol{\theta}} = \int_{\mathbb{T}} p_{\boldsymbol{\theta}}\left(\boldsymbol{\tau}\right)\nabla\log p_{\boldsymbol{\theta}}\left(\boldsymbol{\tau}\right)\nabla\log p_{\boldsymbol{\theta}}\left(\boldsymbol{\tau}\right)^T d\boldsymbol{\tau} = \left\langle\nabla\log p_{\boldsymbol{\theta}}\left(\boldsymbol{\tau}\right)\nabla\log p_{\boldsymbol{\theta}}\left(\boldsymbol{\tau}\right)^T\right\rangle \tag{4.39}$$

is known as the Fisher-information matrix. Let us assume that we fix the amount of change in our policy using the step-size ε. We then have a restricted step-size gradient descent problem (Fletcher & Fletcher, 2000). Thus, we have an optimization problem

$$\max_{\Delta\theta} J\left(\boldsymbol{\theta}+\boldsymbol{\Delta\theta}\right) \approx J\left(\boldsymbol{\theta}\right) + \boldsymbol{\Delta\theta}^T\boldsymbol{\nabla}_{\boldsymbol{\theta}}J, \tag{4.40}$$

$$s.t. d_{\mathrm{KL}}\left(p_{\boldsymbol{\theta}}\left(\boldsymbol{\tau}\right)||p_{\boldsymbol{\theta}+\boldsymbol{\Delta\theta}}\left(\boldsymbol{\tau}\right)\right) \approx \frac{1}{2}\boldsymbol{\Delta\theta}^T\mathbf{F}_{\boldsymbol{\theta}}\,\boldsymbol{\Delta\theta} = \varepsilon, \tag{4.41}$$

which is illustrated in Figure 4.1 and has the solution

$$\boldsymbol{\Delta\theta} = \alpha_n \mathbf{F}_{\boldsymbol{\theta}}^{-1}\boldsymbol{\nabla}_{\boldsymbol{\theta}}J \tag{4.42}$$

with $\alpha_n = [\varepsilon(\nabla J(\boldsymbol{\theta})^T \mathbf{F}_{\boldsymbol{\theta}}^{-1} \nabla J(\boldsymbol{\theta}))^{-1}]^{1/2}$, see Section A.1 for derivations[9]. The direction $\Delta\boldsymbol{\theta}$ is called the natural gradient $\widetilde{\nabla}_{\boldsymbol{\theta}} J(\boldsymbol{\theta}) = \Delta\boldsymbol{\theta}/\alpha_n$ as introduced in (Amari, 1998). The learning rate α_n is not necessarily a desirable one and can be replaced by a constant learning rate without changing the gradient direction.

This type of approach is known as Natural Policy Gradients and has its separate origin in supervised learning (Amari, 1998). It was first suggested in the context of reinforcement learning by Kakade (2002) and has been explored in greater depth in (Peters et al., 2003a; Bagnell & Schneider, 2003; Peters, 2005; Peters et al., 2005). The strongest theoretical advantage of this approach is that its performance no longer depends on the parameterization of the policy and it is therefore safe to use for arbitrary policies[10]. In practice, the learning process converges significantly faster in most practical cases.

4.4.2 Connection to the Compatible Function Approximation

Up to this point, we have left open the deciding question how to determine the Fisher information matrix. In the first work on natural policy gradients (Kakade, 2002), it appeared that this question could not be answered straightforwardly; however this question was largely answered in subsequent work simultaneously by Peters & Schaal, and Bagnell & Schneider, see (Peters et al., 2003a; Bagnell & Schneider, 2003; Peters, 2005; Peters et al., 2005). We repeat our results from (Peters et al., 2003a) and outline the derivation of Fisher information of paths here. In (Moon & Stirling, 2000), we can find the well-known lemma that by differentiating $\int_{\mathbb{T}} p(\boldsymbol{\tau}) d\boldsymbol{\tau} = 1$ twice with respect to the parameters $\boldsymbol{\theta}$, we can obtain

$$\int_{\mathbb{T}} p(\boldsymbol{\tau}) \nabla_{\boldsymbol{\theta}}^2 \log p(\boldsymbol{\tau}) d\boldsymbol{\tau} = -\int_{\mathbb{T}} p(\boldsymbol{\tau}) \nabla_{\boldsymbol{\theta}} \log p(\boldsymbol{\tau}) \nabla_{\boldsymbol{\theta}} \log p(\boldsymbol{\tau})^T d\boldsymbol{\tau} \tag{4.44}$$

for any probability density function $p(\boldsymbol{\tau})$. Using Equations (4.18,4.19), we can obtain by differentiation

$$\nabla_{\boldsymbol{\theta}}^2 \log p(\boldsymbol{\tau}_{0:H}) = \sum_{k=1}^{H} \nabla_{\boldsymbol{\theta}}^2 \log \pi(\mathbf{u}_k | \mathbf{x}_k). \tag{4.45}$$

[9] The value $d_{\mathrm{KL}}(p_{\boldsymbol{\theta}}, p_{\boldsymbol{\theta}+\Delta\boldsymbol{\theta}})$ can also be seen as the *loss of information* resulting of a policy change $\Delta\boldsymbol{\theta}$. Thus, we could alternatively formulate the problem as

$$\max_{\Delta\theta} J(\boldsymbol{\theta} + \Delta\boldsymbol{\theta}) - \alpha d_{\mathrm{KL}}(p_{\boldsymbol{\theta}}, p_{\boldsymbol{\theta}+\Delta\boldsymbol{\theta}}) \approx J(\boldsymbol{\theta}) + \Delta\boldsymbol{\theta}^T \nabla_{\boldsymbol{\theta}} J - \alpha \frac{1}{2} \Delta\boldsymbol{\theta}^T \mathbf{F}_{\boldsymbol{\theta}} \Delta\boldsymbol{\theta}, \tag{4.43}$$

which obviously has the same solution except to the freely selectable trade-off factor or forgetting rate α.

[10] There are a variety of interesting properties to the natural policy gradient methods which are explored in (Peters et al., 2005).

Using Equations (4.44, 4.45), and the definition of the Fisher information matrix (Amari, 1998), we can determine Fisher information matrix for the average reward case in sample notation, i.e,

$$\begin{aligned}
\mathbf{F}_{\boldsymbol{\theta}} &= \left\langle \nabla_{\boldsymbol{\theta}} \log p(\boldsymbol{\tau}_{0:H}) \nabla_{\boldsymbol{\theta}} \log p(\boldsymbol{\tau}_{0:H})^T \right\rangle = -\left\langle \nabla^2_{\boldsymbol{\theta}} \log p(\boldsymbol{\tau}_{0:H}) \right\rangle, \\
&= -\left\langle \sum_{k=0}^{H} \nabla^2_{\boldsymbol{\theta}} \log \pi\left(\mathbf{u}_H \left| \mathbf{x}_H \right.\right) \right\rangle, \\
&= -\int_{\mathbb{X}} d^{\pi}_{H}(\mathbf{x}) \int_{\mathbb{U}} \pi(\mathbf{u}|\mathbf{x}) \nabla^2_{\boldsymbol{\theta}} \log \pi(\mathbf{u}|\mathbf{x}) d\mathbf{u} d\mathbf{x}, \\
&= \int_{\mathbb{X}} d^{\pi}_{H}(\mathbf{x}) \int_{\mathbb{U}} \pi(\mathbf{u}|\mathbf{x}) \nabla_{\boldsymbol{\theta}} \log \pi(\mathbf{u}|\mathbf{x}) \nabla_{\boldsymbol{\theta}} \log \pi(\mathbf{u}|\mathbf{x})^T d\mathbf{u} d\mathbf{x} = \mathbf{G}_{\boldsymbol{\theta}},
\end{aligned} \tag{4.46}$$

where $d^{\pi}_{H}(\mathbf{x}) = \sum_{k=0}^{H} p\left(\mathbf{x}_k = \mathbf{x}\right)$ denotes the distribution of states along the trajectory. Similarly, if we replace $p(\boldsymbol{\tau}_{0:H})$ by a weighted path distribution given by $p_{\gamma}(\boldsymbol{\tau}_{0:n}) = p(\boldsymbol{\tau}_{0:n}) \sum_{l=0}^{H} a_l \mathbb{I}_{x_i,u_i})$, we see that $\nabla^2_{\boldsymbol{\theta}} \log p\left(\boldsymbol{\tau}_{0:n}\right) = \nabla^2_{\boldsymbol{\theta}} \log p_{\gamma}(\boldsymbol{\tau}_{0:n})$. Thus, the proof above generalizes to reweighted path distributions, i.e., we have a state distribution $d^{\pi}_{H}(\mathbf{x}) = \sum_{k=0}^{H} a_k p\left(\mathbf{x}_k = \mathbf{x}\right)$. Thus, we can estimate the Fisher information matrix with

$$\mathbf{F}_{\boldsymbol{\theta}} = \left\langle \sum\nolimits_{l=0}^{H} a_l \nabla_{\boldsymbol{\theta}} \log \pi(\mathbf{u}_l|\mathbf{x}_l) \nabla_{\boldsymbol{\theta}} \log \pi(\mathbf{u}_l|\mathbf{x}_l)^T \right\rangle = \mathbf{G}_{\boldsymbol{\theta}}, \tag{4.47}$$

as we have shown in (Peters et al., 2003a). These results imply the equality of the all-action matrix $\mathbf{G}_{\boldsymbol{\theta}}$ and the Fisher information $\mathbf{F}_{\boldsymbol{\theta}}$ of paths, i.e., we have

$$\mathbf{F}_{\boldsymbol{\theta}} = \mathbf{G}_{\boldsymbol{\theta}}. \tag{4.48}$$

Therefore, we have demonstrated that $F_{\boldsymbol{\theta}}$ is indeed a true Fisher information matrix and does not have to be interpreted as the 'average' of the point Fisher information matrices. Eqs.(4.46) and (4.42) combined imply that the natural gradient can be computed as

$$\widetilde{\nabla}_{\boldsymbol{\theta}} J(\boldsymbol{\theta}) = \mathbf{G}_{\boldsymbol{\theta}}^{-1} \mathbf{F}_{\boldsymbol{\theta}} \mathbf{w} = \mathbf{w}, \tag{4.49}$$

since $\mathbf{F}_{\boldsymbol{\theta}} = \mathbf{G}_{\boldsymbol{\theta}}$. Therefore we only need estimate w and *not* $\mathbf{G}_{\boldsymbol{\theta}}$. The resulting policy improvement step is thus $\boldsymbol{\theta}_{i+1} = \boldsymbol{\theta}_i + \alpha \mathbf{w}$ where α denotes a learning rate.

4.4.3 Natural Actor Critic Algorithms

The critic evaluates the current policy π in order to provide the basis for an actor improvement, i.e., the change $\Delta\boldsymbol{\theta}$ of the policy parameters. As we are interested in natural policy gradient updates $\Delta\boldsymbol{\theta} = \alpha \mathbf{w}$, we wish to employ the compatible function approximation $f^{\pi}_{w}(\mathbf{x}, \mathbf{u})$ from Section 4.3.3 in this context. In Section 4.3.3, we had realized that this function was hard to learn as it could only represent an impoverished version of the state-action value function. We will remedy this situation we will derive more useful

Table 4.5: Natural Actor-Critic Algorithm with LSTD-Q(λ)

input: policy parameterization $\boldsymbol{\theta}$
if first gradient estimate
reset sufficient statistics $\mathbf{A}_0 = \mathbf{0}$, $\mathbf{b}_0 = \mathbf{z}_0 = \mathbf{0}$, $k = 0$.
else
forget statistics: $\mathbf{z}_{k+1} \leftarrow 0$, $\mathbf{A}_{k+1} \leftarrow \beta \mathbf{A}_{k+1}$, $\mathbf{b}_{k+1} \leftarrow \beta \mathbf{b}_{k+1}$.
end.
repeat
Draw initial state $\mathbf{x}_0 \sim p(\mathbf{x}_0)$.
for $t = 0, 1, 2, \ldots, H$ **do**
Execute a step:
Draw action $\mathbf{u}_t \sim \pi(\mathbf{u}_t \mid \mathbf{x}_t)$.
Observe next state $\mathbf{x}_{t+1} \sim p(\mathbf{x}_{t+1} \mid \mathbf{x}_t, \mathbf{u}_t)$.
Observe reward $r_t = r(\mathbf{x}_t, \mathbf{u}_t)$.
Update basis functions:
$\widetilde{\boldsymbol{\phi}}_t = [\boldsymbol{\phi}(\mathbf{x}_{t+1})^T, \mathbf{0}^T]^T$,
$\widehat{\boldsymbol{\phi}}_t = [\boldsymbol{\phi}(\mathbf{x}_t)^T, \boldsymbol{\nabla}_{\boldsymbol{\theta}} \log \pi(\mathbf{u}_t \mid \mathbf{x}_t)^T]^T$,
Update sufficient statistics:
$\mathbf{z}_{k+1} = \lambda \mathbf{z}_k + \widehat{\boldsymbol{\phi}}_t$,
$\mathbf{A}_{k+1} = \mathbf{A}_k + \mathbf{z}_{k+1}(\widehat{\boldsymbol{\phi}}_t - \gamma \widetilde{\boldsymbol{\phi}}_t)^T$,
$\mathbf{b}_{k+1} = \mathbf{b}_k + \mathbf{z}_{k+1} r_t$,
Update critic parameters: $[\mathbf{w}_{k+1}^T, \mathbf{v}_{k+1}^T]^T = \mathbf{A}_{k+1}^{-1} \mathbf{b}_{k+1}$.
Update time-step $k \leftarrow k + 1$.
end for.
until gradient estimate $\mathbf{g}_{\mathrm{NAC}} = \mathbf{w}_k$ converged.
return: gradient estimate $\mathbf{g}_{\mathrm{NAC}} = \mathbf{w}_k$

estimators from two different point of views, i.e., the state-action based point of view and the episodic roll-out based point of view. Both rely on the assumption of additional basis functions.

4.4.3.1 Natural Actor Critic with LSTD-Q(λ)

We observe that we can write the Bellman equations (e.g., see (Baird, 1993)) in terms of the advantage function and the state-value function

$$Q^\pi(\mathbf{x}, \mathbf{u}) = A^\pi(\mathbf{x}, \mathbf{u}) + V^\pi(\mathbf{x}) = r(\mathbf{x}, \mathbf{u}) + \gamma \int_{\mathbb{X}} p(\mathbf{x}' \mid \mathbf{x}, \mathbf{u}) V^\pi(\mathbf{x}') d\mathbf{x}'. \quad (4.50)$$

Inserting $A^{\pi}(\mathbf{x},\mathbf{u}) = f_w^{\pi}(\mathbf{x},\mathbf{u})$ and an appropriate basis functions representation of the value function as $V^{\pi}(\mathbf{x}) = \boldsymbol{\phi}(\mathbf{x})^T\mathbf{v}$, we can rewrite the Bellman Equation, Equation , (4.50), as a set of linear equations

$$\nabla_{\boldsymbol{\theta}} \log \pi(\mathbf{u}_t|\mathbf{x}_t)^T\mathbf{w} + \boldsymbol{\phi}(\mathbf{x}_t)^T\mathbf{v} = r(\mathbf{x}_t,\mathbf{u}_t) + \gamma\boldsymbol{\phi}(\mathbf{x}_{t+1})^T\mathbf{v} + \epsilon(\mathbf{x}_t,\mathbf{u}_t,\mathbf{x}_{t+1}) \quad (4.51)$$

where $\epsilon(\mathbf{x}_t,\mathbf{u}_t,\mathbf{x}_{t+1})$ denotes an error term which mean-zero as can be observed from Equation (4.50). Using Equation (4.51), a solution to Equation (4.50) can be obtained by adapting the LSTD(λ) policy evaluation algorithm (Boyan, 1999). For this purpose, we define

$$\begin{aligned} \widehat{\boldsymbol{\phi}}_t &= [\boldsymbol{\phi}(\mathbf{x}_t)^T, \nabla_{\boldsymbol{\theta}} \log \pi(\mathbf{u}_t|\mathbf{x}_t)^T]^T, \\ \widetilde{\boldsymbol{\phi}}_t &= [\boldsymbol{\phi}(\mathbf{x}_{t+1})^T, \mathbf{0}^T]^T, \end{aligned} \quad (4.52)$$

as new basis functions, where $\mathbf{0}$ is the zero vector. This definition of basis function reduces bias and variance of the learning process in comparison to SARSA and previous LSTD(λ) algorithms for state-action value functions (Boyan, 1999) as the basis functions $\widetilde{\boldsymbol{\phi}}_t$ do not depend on stochastic future actions $\mathbf{u}_{t+1}$, i.e., the input variables to the LSTD regression are not noisy due to $\mathbf{u}_{t+1}$ (e.g., as in (Bradtke, Ydstie, & Barto, 1994)) – such input noise would violate the standard regression model that only takes noise in the regression targets into account. LSTD(λ) with the basis functions in Equation (4.52), called LSTD-Q(λ) from now on, is thus currently the theoretically cleanest way of applying LSTD to state-value function estimation. It is exact for deterministic or weekly noisy state transitions and arbitrary stochastic policies. As all previous LSTD suggestions, it loses accuracy with increasing noise in the state transitions since $\widetilde{\boldsymbol{\phi}}_t$ becomes a random variable. The complete LSTD-Q(λ) algorithm is given in the *Critic Evaluation* (lines 12-17) of Table 4.5.

Once LSTD-Q(λ) converges to an approximation of $A^{\pi}(\mathbf{x}_t,\mathbf{u}_t) + V^{\pi}(\mathbf{x}_t)$, we obtain two results: the value function parameters $\mathbf{v}$, and the natural gradient $\mathbf{w}$. The natural gradient $\mathbf{w}$ serves in updating the policy parameters $\Delta\boldsymbol{\theta}_t = \alpha\mathbf{w}_t$. After this update, the critic has to forget at least parts of its accumulated sufficient statistics using a forgetting factor $\beta \in [0,1]$ (cf. Table 4.5). For $\beta = 0$, i.e., complete resetting, and appropriate basis functions $\phi(\mathbf{x})$, convergence to the true natural gradient can be guaranteed. The complete Natural Actor Critic (NAC) algorithm is shown in Table 4.5.

However, it becomes fairly obvious that the basis functions can have an influence on our gradient estimate. When using the counterexample in (Bartlett, 2002) with a typical Gibbs policy, we will realize that the gradient is affected for $\lambda < 1$; for $\lambda = 0$ the gradient is flipped and would always worsen the policy. Thus, it would result in a biased gradient update for $\lambda < 1$, however, unlike in (Bartlett, 2002), we at least could guarantee that the gradient is unbiased for $\lambda = 1$.

Table 4.6: Episodic Natural Actor Critic

input: policy parameterization $\boldsymbol{\theta}$.	
1	**repeat**
2	perform M trials and obtain $\mathbf{x}_{0:H}, \mathbf{u}_{0:H}, r_{0:H}$ for each trial.
	Obtain the sufficient statistics
3	Policy derivatives $\boldsymbol{\psi}_k = \boldsymbol{\nabla}_\theta \log \pi_{\boldsymbol{\theta}} (\mathbf{u}_k \| \mathbf{x}_k)$.
4	Fisher matrix $\mathbf{F}_{\boldsymbol{\theta}} = \left\langle \left(\sum_{k=0}^{H} \boldsymbol{\psi}_k\right) \left(\sum_{l=0}^{H} \boldsymbol{\psi}_l\right)^T \right\rangle$.
	Vanilla gradient $\mathbf{g} = \left\langle \left(\sum_{k=0}^{H} \boldsymbol{\psi}_k\right) \left(\sum_{l=0}^{H} a_l r_l\right) \right\rangle$.
5	Eligbility $\boldsymbol{\phi} = \left\langle \left(\sum_{k=0}^{H} \boldsymbol{\psi}_k\right) \right\rangle$.
6	Average reward $\bar{r} = \left\langle \sum_{l=0}^{H} a_l r_l \right\rangle$.
	Obtain natural gradient by computing
7	Baseline $b = \mathbf{Q}\left(\bar{r} - \boldsymbol{\phi}^T \mathbf{F}_{\boldsymbol{\theta}}^{-1} \mathbf{g}\right)$
	with $\mathbf{Q} = M^{-1}\left(1 + \boldsymbol{\phi}^T \left(M\mathbf{F}_{\boldsymbol{\theta}} - \boldsymbol{\phi}\boldsymbol{\phi}^T\right)^{-1} \boldsymbol{\phi}\right)$
8	Natural gradient $\mathbf{g}_{\text{eNAC1}} = \mathbf{F}_{\boldsymbol{\theta}}^{-1} (\mathbf{g} - \boldsymbol{\phi} b)$.
9	**until** gradient estimate $\mathbf{g}_{\text{eNAC1}}$ converged.
return: gradient estimate $\mathbf{g}_{\text{eNAC1}}$.	

4.4.3.2 Episodic Natural Actor-Critic

Given the problem that the additional basis functions $\phi(\mathbf{x})$ determine the quality of the gradient, we need methods which guarantee the unbiasedness of the natural gradient estimate. Such method can be determined by summing up Equation (4.51) along a sample path, we obtain

$$\sum_{t=0}^{H} a_t A^\pi(\mathbf{x}_t, \mathbf{u}_t) = a_{H+1} V^\pi(\mathbf{x}_{H+1}) + \sum_{t=0}^{H} a_t r(\mathbf{x}_t, \mathbf{u}_t) - V^\pi(\mathbf{x}_0) \tag{4.53}$$

It is fairly obvious that the last term disappears for $H \to \infty$ or episodic tasks (where $r(\mathbf{x}_H, \mathbf{u}_H)$ is the final reward); therefore each roll-out would yield one equation. If we furthermore assume a single start-state, an additional scalar value function of $\phi(x) = 1$ suffices. We therefore get a straightforward regression problem:

$$\sum_{t=0}^{H} a_t \boldsymbol{\nabla} \log \pi(\mathbf{u}_t, \mathbf{x}_t)^T \mathbf{w} + J = \sum_{t=0}^{H} a_t r(\mathbf{x}_t, \mathbf{u}_t) \tag{4.54}$$

with exactly $\dim\theta + 1$ unknowns. This means that for non-stochastic tasks we can obtain a natural gradient after $\dim\theta + 1$ rollouts using least squares regression

$$\begin{bmatrix} \mathbf{w} \\ J \end{bmatrix} = \left(\Psi^T \Psi\right)^{-1} \Psi^T \mathbf{R}, \tag{4.55}$$

with

$$\Psi_i = \left[\sum_{t=0}^{H} a_t \nabla \log \pi(\mathbf{u}_t, \mathbf{x}_t)^T, 1 \right], \tag{4.56}$$

$$\mathbf{R}_i = \sum_{t=0}^{H} a_t r(\mathbf{x}_t, \mathbf{u}_t). \tag{4.57}$$

This regression problem, can be transformed into the form shown shown in Table 4.6 using the matrix inversion lemmata, see Section A.4.1 for the derivation.

This algorithm, originally derived in (Peters, 2005; Peters et al., 2003a, 2005), can be considered the 'natural' version of reinforce with a baseline optimal for this gradient estimator. However, for steepest descent with respect to a metric, the baseline also needs to minimize the variance with respect to the same metric and, thus, the episodic natural actor critic can be derived similar as the normal likelihood ratio gradients before. In this case, we can minimize the whole covariance matrix of the natural gradient estimate $\Delta\hat{\boldsymbol{\theta}}$ given by

$$\begin{aligned} \Sigma &= \operatorname{Cov}\left\{\Delta\hat{\boldsymbol{\theta}}\right\}_{\mathbf{F}_{\boldsymbol{\theta}}} \\ &= E\left\{\left(\Delta\hat{\boldsymbol{\theta}} - \mathbf{F}_{\boldsymbol{\theta}}^{-1}\mathbf{g}_{\mathrm{RF}}(b)\right)^T \mathbf{F}_{\boldsymbol{\theta}} \left(\Delta\hat{\boldsymbol{\theta}} - \mathbf{F}_{\boldsymbol{\theta}}^{-1}\mathbf{g}_{\mathrm{RF}}(b)\right)\right\}, \end{aligned}$$

with $\mathbf{g}_{\mathrm{RF}}(b) = \langle \nabla \log p_{\boldsymbol{\theta}}(\boldsymbol{\tau})\left(r(\boldsymbol{\tau}) - b\right)\rangle$ being the REINFORCE gradient with baseline b. As outlined in (Peters, 2005; Peters et al., 2003a, 2005), it can be shown that the minimum-variance unbiased natural gradient estimator.

4.4.3.3 Episodic Natural Actor Critic with a Time-Variant Baseline

The episodic natural actor critic described in the previous section suffers from drawback: it does not make use of intermediate data just like REINFORCE. For policy gradients, the way out was G(PO)MDP which left out terms which would average out in expectation. In the same manner, we can make the argument for a time-dependent baseline which then allows us to reformulate the Episodic Natural Actor Critic. This argument results in the algorithm shown in Table 4.7 and the derivation is shown in Section A.4.2. The advantage of this type of algorithms is two-fold: the variance of the gradient estimate is often lower and it can take time-variant rewards significantly better into account.

Table 4.7: Episodic Natural Actor Critic with a Time-Variant Baseline

input: policy parameterization $\boldsymbol{\theta}$.	
1	**repeat**
2	perform M trials and obtain $\mathbf{x}_{0:H}, \mathbf{u}_{0:H}, r_{0:H}$ for each trial.
	Obtain the sufficient statistics
3	Policy derivatives $\boldsymbol{\psi}_k = \boldsymbol{\nabla}_\theta \log \pi_{\boldsymbol{\theta}} (\mathbf{u}_k \| \mathbf{x}_k)$.
4	Fisher matrix $\mathbf{F}_{\boldsymbol{\theta}} = \left\langle \sum_{k=0}^{H} \left(\sum_{l=0}^{k} \boldsymbol{\psi}_l \right) \boldsymbol{\psi}_k^T \right\rangle$.
	Vanilla gradient $\mathbf{g} = \left\langle \sum_{k=0}^{H} \left(\sum_{l=0}^{k} \boldsymbol{\psi}_l \right) a_k r_k \right\rangle$,
5	Eligbility matrix $\boldsymbol{\Phi} = [\boldsymbol{\phi}_1, \boldsymbol{\phi}_2, \ldots, \boldsymbol{\phi}_K]$
	with $\boldsymbol{\phi}_h = \left\langle \left(\sum_{k=0}^{h} \boldsymbol{\psi}_k \right) \right\rangle$.
6	Average reward vector $\bar{\mathbf{r}} = [\bar{r}_1, \bar{r}_2, \ldots, \bar{r}_K]$
	with $\bar{r}_h = \langle a_h r_h \rangle$.
	Obtain natural gradient by computing
7	Baseline $\mathbf{b} = \mathbf{Q} \left(\bar{\mathbf{r}} - \boldsymbol{\Phi}^T \mathbf{F}_{\boldsymbol{\theta}}^{-1} \mathbf{g} \right)$
	with $\mathbf{Q} = M^{-1} \left(\mathbf{I}_K + \boldsymbol{\Phi}^T \left(M \mathbf{F}_{\boldsymbol{\theta}} - \boldsymbol{\Phi} \boldsymbol{\Phi}^T \right)^{-1} \boldsymbol{\Phi} \right)$.
8	Natural gradient $\mathbf{g}_{\mathrm{NG}} = \mathbf{F}_{\boldsymbol{\theta}}^{-1} \left(\mathbf{g} - \boldsymbol{\Phi} \mathbf{b} \right)$.
9	**until** gradient estimate $\mathbf{g}_{\mathrm{eNACn}}$ converged.
return: gradient estimate $\mathbf{g}_{\mathrm{eNACn}}$.	

4.5 Properties of Natural Actor-Critic

In this section, we will emphasize certain properties of the natural actor-critic. In particular, we want to give a simple proof of covariance of the natural policy gradient, and discuss (Kakade, 2002) observation that in his experimental settings the natural policy gradient was non-covariant. Furthermore, we will discuss another surprising aspect about the Natural Actor-Critic (NAC) which is its relation to previous algorithms. We briefly demonstrate that established algorithms like the classic Actor-Critic (Sutton & Barto, 1998), and Bradtke's Q-Learning (Bradtke et al., 1994) can be seen as special cases of NAC.

4.5.1 On the Covariance of Natural Policy Gradients

When (Kakade, 2002) originally suggested natural policy gradients, he came to the disappointing conclusion that they were not covariant. As counterexample, he suggested that for two different linear Gaussian policies, (one in the normal form, and the other in the information form) the probability distributions represented by the natural policy gradient would be affected differently, i.e., the natural policy gradient would be non-covariant. We intend to give a proof at this point showing that the natural policy gradient is in fact covariant under certain conditions, and clarify why (Kakade, 2002) experienced these difficulties.

Theorem 4.1 *Natural policy gradients updates are covariant for two policies $\pi_{\boldsymbol{\theta}}$ parameterized by $\boldsymbol{\theta}$ and $\pi_{\mathbf{h}}$ parameterized by $\mathbf{h}$ if (i) for all parameters θ_i there exists a function $\theta_i = f_i(h_1, \ldots, h_k)$, (ii) the derivative $\nabla_{\mathbf{h}}\boldsymbol{\theta}$ and its inverse $\nabla_{\mathbf{h}}\boldsymbol{\theta}^{-1}$, and (iii) there are no redundant parameters (i.e., the Fisher information matrix is non-singular).*

For the proof see Appendix A.2. Practical experiments show that the problems occurred for Gaussian policies in (Kakade, 2002) are in fact due to the selection the stepsize α which determines the length of $\Delta\boldsymbol{\theta}$. As the linearization $\Delta\boldsymbol{\theta} = \nabla_{\mathbf{h}}\boldsymbol{\theta}^T\Delta\mathbf{h}$ does not hold for large $\Delta\boldsymbol{\theta}$, this can cause divergence between the algorithms even for analytically determined natural policy gradients which can partially explain the difficulties occurred by Kakade (Kakade, 2002).

4.5.2 NAC's Relation to previous Algorithms

Original Actor-Critic. Surprisingly, the original Actor-Critic algorithm (Sutton & Barto, 1998) is a form of the Natural Actor-Critic. By choosing a Gibbs policy

$$\pi(u_t|x_t) = \frac{\exp(\theta_{xu})}{\sum_b \exp(\theta_{xb})}, \tag{4.58}$$

with all parameters θ_{xu} lumped in the vector $\boldsymbol{\theta}$, (denoted as $\boldsymbol{\theta} = [\theta_{xu}]$) in a discrete setup with tabular representations of transition probabilities and rewards. A linear function approximation $V^\pi(x) = \boldsymbol{\phi}(x)^T\mathbf{v}$ with $\mathbf{v} = [v_x]$ and unit basis functions $\boldsymbol{\phi}(x) = \mathbf{e}_x$ was employed. Sutton et al. online update rule is given by

$$\begin{aligned}
\theta_{xu}^{t+1} &= \theta_{xu}^t + \alpha_1 \left(r(x,u) + \gamma v_{x'} - v_x\right), \\
v_x^{t+1} &= v_x^t + \alpha_2 \left(r(x,u) + \gamma v_{x'} - v_x\right),
\end{aligned}$$

where α_1, α_2 denote learning rates. The update of the critic parameters v_x^t equals the one of the Natural Actor-Critic in expectation as TD(0) critics converges to the same values as LSTD(0) and LSTD-Q(0) for discrete problems (Boyan, 1999). Since for the Gibbs policy we have

$$\frac{\partial \log \pi(b|a)}{\partial \theta_{xu}} = \begin{cases} 1 - \pi(b|a) & \text{if } \; a = x \text{ and } b = u, \\ -\pi(b|a) & \text{if } \; a = x \text{ and } b \neq u, \\ 0 & \text{otherwise,} \end{cases} \tag{4.59}$$

and as $\sum_b \pi(b|x)A(x,b) = 0$, we can evaluate the advantage function and derive

$$A(x,u) = A(x,u) - \sum\nolimits_b \pi(b|x)A(x,b) = \sum\nolimits_b \frac{\partial \log \pi(b|x)}{\partial \theta_{xu}} A(x,b).$$

Since the compatible function approximation represents the advantage function, i.e., $f^{\pi}_{\mathbf{w}}(\mathbf{x}, \mathbf{u}) = A(x, u)$, we realize that the advantages equal the natural gradient, i.e., $\mathbf{w} = [A(x, u)]$. Furthermore, the TD(0) error of a state-action pair (x, u) equals the advantage function in expectation, and therefore the natural gradient update

$$w_{xu} = A(x, u) = E_{x'}\{r(x, u) + \gamma V(x') - V(x)|x, u\}, \quad (4.60)$$

corresponds to the average online updates of Actor-Critic. As both update rules of the Actor-Critic correspond to the ones of NAC, we can see both algorithms as equivalent.

Bradtke's Q-Learning. Bradtke et al. (1994) proposed an algorithm with the policy $\pi(u_t|\mathbf{x}_t) = \mathcal{N}(u_t|\mathbf{k}_i^T\mathbf{x}_t, \sigma_i^2)$ and parameters $\boldsymbol{\theta}_i = [\mathbf{k}_i^T, \sigma_i]^T$ (where σ_i denotes the exploration, and i the policy update time step) in a linear control task with linear state transitions $\mathbf{x}_{t+1} = \mathbf{A}\mathbf{x}_t + \mathbf{b}u_t$, and quadratic rewards $r(\mathbf{x}_t, \mathbf{u}_t) = \mathbf{x}_t^T\mathbf{H}\mathbf{x}_t + Ru_t^2$. They evaluated $Q^{\pi}(\mathbf{x}_t, \mathbf{u}_t)$ with LSTD(0) using a quadratic polynomial expansion as basis functions, and applied greedy updates:

$$\mathbf{k}_{i+1}^{\text{Bradtke}} = \text{argmax}_{\mathbf{k}_{i+1}} Q^{\pi}(\mathbf{x}_t, \mathbf{u}_t = \mathbf{k}_{i+1}^T\mathbf{x}_t) = -(R + \gamma\mathbf{b}^T\mathbf{P}_i\mathbf{b})^{-1}\gamma\mathbf{b}\mathbf{P}_i\mathbf{A},$$

where $\mathbf{P}_i$ denotes policy-specific value function parameters related to the gain $\mathbf{k}_i$; no update the exploration σ_i was included. Similarly, we can obtain the natural policy gradient $\mathbf{w} = [\mathbf{w}_{\mathbf{k}}, w_{\sigma}]^T$, as yielded by LSTD-Q($\lambda$) analytically using the compatible function approximation and the same quadratic basis functions. As discussed in detail in (Peters et al., 2003a), this gives us

$$\mathbf{w}_{\mathbf{k}} = (\gamma\mathbf{A}^T\mathbf{P}_i\mathbf{b} + (R + \gamma\mathbf{b}^T\mathbf{P}_i\mathbf{b})\mathbf{k})^T\sigma_i^2,$$
$$w_{\sigma} = 0.5(\mathbf{R} + \gamma\mathbf{b}^T\mathbf{P}_i\mathbf{b})\sigma_i^3.$$

Similarly, it can be derived that the expected return is $J(\boldsymbol{\theta}_i) = -(R + \gamma\mathbf{b}^T\mathbf{P}_i\mathbf{b})\sigma_i^2$ for this type of problems, see (Peters et al., 2003a). For a learning rate $\alpha_i = 1/\|J(\boldsymbol{\theta}_i)\|$, we see

$$\mathbf{k}_{i+1} = \mathbf{k}_i + \alpha_t\mathbf{w}_{\mathbf{k}} = \mathbf{k}_i - (\mathbf{k}_i + (R + \gamma\mathbf{b}^T\mathbf{P}_i\mathbf{b})^{-1}\gamma\mathbf{A}^T\mathbf{P}_i\mathbf{b}) = \mathbf{k}_{i+1}^{\text{Bradtke}},$$

which demonstrates that *Bradtke's Actor Update is a special case of the Natural Actor-Critic*. NAC extends Bradtke's result as it gives an update rule for the exploration – which was not possible in Bradtke's greedy framework.

4.6 Experiments & Results

In the previous section, we outlined the five first-order, model-free policy gradient algorithms which are most relevant for robotics (further ones exist but are do not scale

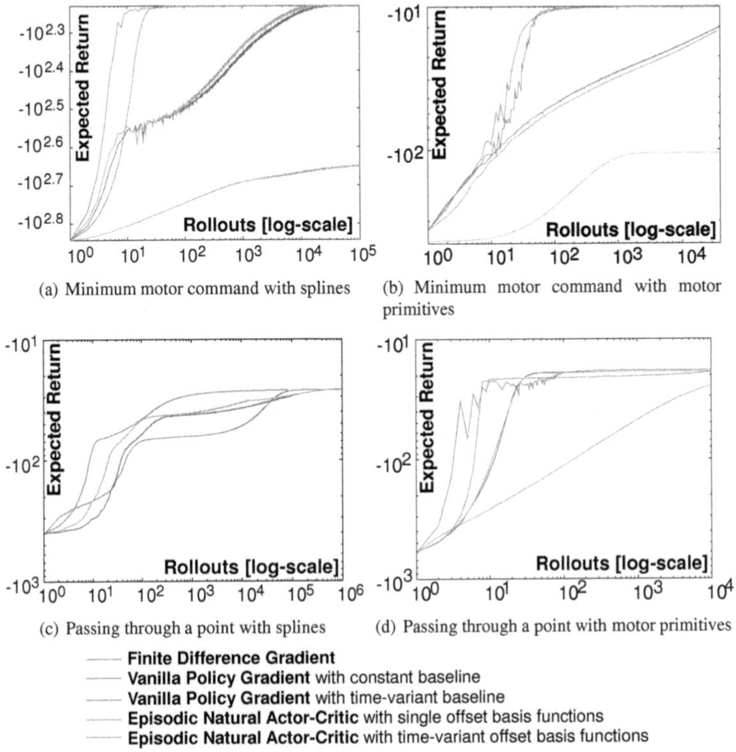

(a) Minimum motor command with splines

(b) Minimum motor command with motor primitives

(c) Passing through a point with splines

(d) Passing through a point with motor primitives

(e) Legend

Figure 4.2: This figure shows different experiments with motor task learning. In (a,b), we see how the learning system creates minimum motor command goal-achieving plans using both (a) splines and (b) motor primitives. For this problem, the natural actor-critic methods beat all other methods by several orders of magnitude. In (c,d), the plan has to achieve an intermediary goal. While the natural actor-critic methods still outperform previous methods, the gap is lower as the learning problem is easier. Note that these are double logarithmic plots.

into high-dimensional robot domains). In this section, we will demonstrate how these different algorithms compare in practice in different areas relevant to robotics. For this pupose, we will show experiments on both simulated plants as well as on real robots and we will compare the algorithms for the optimization of control laws and for learning of motor skills.

4.6.1 Comparing Policy Gradient Methods on Motor Primitives

Initially, we compare the different policy gradient methods in motor primitive planning tasks using both spline-based and dynamical system based desired trajectories. In Figure 4.2 (a) and (b), we show a comparison of the presented algorithms for a simple, single DOF task with a reward of

$$r_k(x_{0:N}, u_{0:N}) = \sum_{i=0}^{N} c_1 \dot{q}_{d,k,i}^2 + c_2(q_{d;k;N} - g_k)^2 \tag{4.61}$$

where $c_1 = 1$, $c_2 = 1000$ for both splines and dynamic motor primitives. In Figure 4.2 (c) and (d) we show the same with an additional punishment term for going through a intermediate point p_F at time F, i.e.,

$$r_k(x_{0:N}, u_{0:N}) = \sum_{i=0}^{N} \tilde{c}_1 \dot{q}_{d,k,i}^2 + \tilde{c}_2(q_{d;k;N} - g_k)^2 + \tilde{c}_2(q_{d;F;N} - p_F)^2. \tag{4.62}$$

It is quite clear from the results that the natural actor-critic methods outperform both the vanilla policy gradient methods as well as the likelihood ratio methods. Finite difference gradient methods behave differently from the likelihood ratio methods as there is no stochasticity in the system, resulting in a cleaner gradient but also in local minima not present for likelihood ratio methods where the exploratory actions are stochastic. From this comparison, we can conclude that natural actor-critic methods are the best suited for motor primitive learning.

4.6.2 Robot Application: Motor Primitive Learning for Baseball

We also evaluated the same setup in a challenging robot task, i.e., the planning of these motor primitives for a seven DOF robot task using our SARCOS Master Arm. The task of the robot is to hit the ball properly so that it flies as far as possible; this game is also known as T-Ball. The state of the robot is given by its joint angles and velocities while the action are the joint accelerations. The reward is extracted using color segment tracking with a NewtonLabs vision system. Initially, we teach a rudimentary stroke by supervised learning as can be seen in Figure 4.3 (b); however, it fails to reproduce the behavior as shown in (c); subsequently, we improve the performance using the episodic

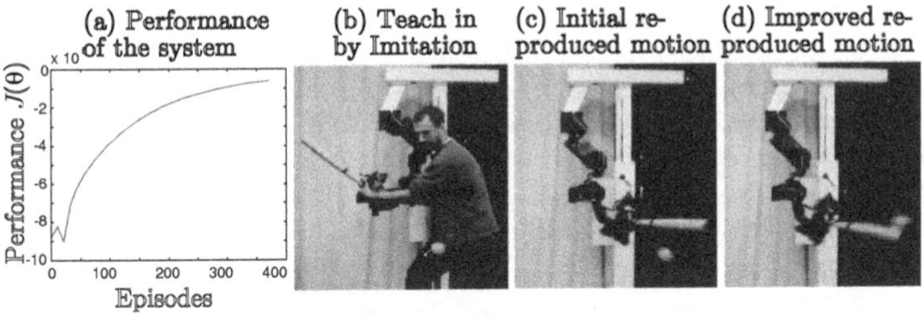

Figure 4.3: This figure shows (a) the performance of a baseball swing task when using the motor primitives for learning. In (b), the learning system is initialized by imitation learning, in (c) it is initially failing at reproducing the motor behavior, and (d) after several hundred episodes exhibiting a nicely learned batting.

Natural Actor-Critic which yields the performance shown in (a) and the behavior in (d). After approximately 200-300 trials, the ball can be hit properly by the robot.

4.7 Conclusion & Discussion

The contributions of this chapter are outlined in Section 4.7.1, and we discuss the relations between policy gradient and extensions of the EM-like approaches in Section 4.7.2. Furthermore, in Section 4.7.3, we discuss a new approach tailored for motor primitive learning, i.e., the motor primitive iteration.

4.7.1 Contributions of this Chapter

We have presented an extensive survey of policy gradient methods. While some developments needed to be omitted as they are only applicable for very low-dimensional state-spaces, this book chapter represents the state of the art in policy gradient methods and can deliver a solid base for future applications of policy gradient methods in robotics. All three major ways of estimating first order gradients, i.e., finite-difference gradients, vanilla policy gradients and natural policy gradients are discussed in this book chapter and practical algorithms are given.

One of the presented classes of algorithms, the Natural Actor-Critic algorithms were developed for this book. While developed in the beginning of the Ph.D. of the author, these algorithms have been widely accepted by now and have been applied in a variety of settings (Guenter, Hersch, Calinon, & Billard, 2007; Mori, Nakamura, & Ishii, 2005; Mori et al., 2004; Nakamura et al., 2004; Park, Kim, & Kang, 2005; Richter, Aberdeen, & Yu, 2007; Sato et al., 2002; Ueno et al., 2006). The Natural Actor-Critic is considered **"Current method of choice"** (Aberdeen, 2006) among the policy gradient in the reinforcement learning community. It also allows the derivation of several previous algorithms and has very useful properties.

The experiments presented here show that the time-variant episodic natural actor critic is the preferred method among the presented methods when applicable; however, if a policy cannot be differentiated with respect to its parameters, the finite difference methods may be the only method applicable. The example of motor primitive learning for baseball underlines the efficiency of natural gradient methods.

4.7.2 Relation to EM-based Approaches

Interestingly, the methods used for immediate reinforcement learning in Section 3.3 are related to policy gradient approaches and can be extended to trajectories. For this, let us discuss this topic without considering the adaptive reward transformation, i.e., the presented EM-like algorithm could be derived from

$$\boldsymbol{\theta}_{k+1} = \mathrm{argmax}_{\boldsymbol{\theta}'}\, d_{\mathrm{KL}}\left(p_{\boldsymbol{\theta}_k}(\boldsymbol{\tau})\, r(\boldsymbol{\tau}) \| \, p_{\boldsymbol{\theta}'}(\boldsymbol{\tau})\right), \tag{4.63}$$

which can be shown to maximize the lower bound on $J(\theta) = \int p_{\boldsymbol{\theta}}(\boldsymbol{\tau})\, r(\boldsymbol{\tau})\, d\boldsymbol{\tau}$ in the same fashion as shown in Section 3.3. While the EM solution yields a parameter free one-step improvement, we can also look at the gradient of $d_{\mathrm{KL}}(p_{\boldsymbol{\theta}_k}(\boldsymbol{\tau})\, r(\boldsymbol{\tau})\, || p_{\boldsymbol{\theta}'}(\boldsymbol{\tau}))$ which is used in the EM-update. This analysis yields

$$\frac{d}{d\boldsymbol{\theta}'} d_{\mathrm{KL}}\left(p_{\boldsymbol{\theta}_k}(\boldsymbol{\tau})\, r(\boldsymbol{\tau}) \| \, p_{\boldsymbol{\theta}'}(\boldsymbol{\tau})\right) \tag{4.64}$$

$$= \frac{d}{d\boldsymbol{\theta}'} \int_{\mathbb{T}} p_{\boldsymbol{\theta}_k}(\boldsymbol{\tau})\, r(\boldsymbol{\tau}) \log \frac{p_{\boldsymbol{\theta}'}(\boldsymbol{\tau})}{p_{\boldsymbol{\theta}_k}(\boldsymbol{\tau})\, r(\boldsymbol{\tau})} d\boldsymbol{\tau}, \tag{4.65}$$

$$= \int_{\mathbb{T}} p_{\boldsymbol{\theta}_k}(\boldsymbol{\tau})\, r(\boldsymbol{\tau}) \frac{d}{d\boldsymbol{\theta}'} \log p_{\boldsymbol{\theta}'}(\boldsymbol{\tau})\, d\boldsymbol{\tau} = \boldsymbol{\nabla}_{\boldsymbol{\theta}} J(\theta), \tag{4.66}$$

i.e., it shows that the vanilla policy gradient is used in EM-like approaches. In pratice, the EM-like algorithms usually choose very conservative updates and simple evaluations on toy problems for episodic reinforcement learning show that the EM-like RL algorithms are very sensitive to the data distribution. Thus, when applied to trajectories, the natural actor-critic outperforms vanilla EM-like methods significantly. However, it is obvious that extensions with appropriate constraints can be of significant advantage here, especially if the reduction onto regression is being used as in Section 3.3. Thus, this remains an important topic for future research.

4.7.3 Future Work: Motor Primitive Iteration

In this chapter, we have focussed on the application of model free, general policy gradient approaches. Alternatives arise for learning motor primitives for the framework suggested in (Ijspeert et al., 2002, 2003). In this framework, we have two second-order linear systems coupled through a locally weighted linear function approximator. For this reason, one could look at the nonlinear system

$$\dot{\mathbf{x}} = \mathbf{A}_x\mathbf{x} + \mathbf{e}_2 f\left(y\right) = \mathbf{A}\mathbf{x} + \mathbf{B}\mathbf{u}, \tag{4.67}$$

as a linear system with the coupling $\mathbf{u} = f\left(y\right)$ to the canonical system $\mathbf{y}$ as optimal controls. As this coupling is implemented through a locally linear weighted function approximator such as

$$f\left(y\right) = \frac{\sum_{i=1}^{n} \phi_i\left(y\right) w_i^T y}{\sum_{i=1}^{n} \phi_i\left(y\right)},$$

it is logical, that the reward should also be approximated locally in a similar fashion, e.g., through approximations of the reward using the same local weightings such as

$$r\left(y, x, u\right) = \frac{\sum_{i=1}^{n} \phi_i\left(y\right) \left[R_i\left(u - u_i\right)^2 + Q_i\left(x - x_i\right)^2\right]}{\sum_{i=1}^{n} \phi_i\left(y\right)}. \tag{4.68}$$

In this case, there would be two natural steps, i.e., (i) a motor primitive policy evaluations step where several rollouts would allow the learning of the local parameters, e.g., R_i, Q_i, u_i, x_i, and (ii) a policy improvement step which would compute the optimal controls based on these parameters. The optimal controls would then serve as supervised learning targets in order to determine the motor primitive parameters. If necessary, Gallerkin solution methods could allow an extensing to cases beyond the capabilities of traditional optimal control methods (Beard & McLain, 1998). This method could serve as a promising new method specifically for motor primitives but would of course always be limited to motor primitive learning.

Chapter 5

Conclusion

Reasoning draws a conclusion,
but does not make the conclusion certain,
unless the mind discovers it by the path of experience.
Roger Bacon (English empiricist, 1214 - 1294)

This book has been about the greater goal of creating a general machine learning framework for acquiring and improving motor skills in robotics. Several important contributions in the areas of learning, motor skills and robotics have been made which bring us a step closer to that ultimate aim. In this chapter, we will first summarize the insights and results of this book. Subsequently, we discuss the different approaches as well the important next steps needed in order to solve the general problem of motor skill learning.

5.1 Summary of the Contributions

In this book, we have presented several different contributions to three different but interrelated topics, i.e., machine learning (particularly reinforcement learning), motor skill representation and control as well as robot applications. The main results of this book have been grouped into three chapters which are written in such a way that they can be read independently of each other. However, following the sequence of these chapters will help the understanding of the single chapters tremendously.

In Chapter 1, we have given an introduction of the book. This chapter started with the general motivation of the chosen topic, i.e., *Machine Learning for Motor Skills in Robotics*. It included a summary of the most important novel developments which we have presented in the following chapters and an outline of the remainder of the book.

In Chapter 2, we started with the seminal work of Udwadia (1996, 2003) on the relation between analytical dynamics and control. The underlying key insight is that Nature enforces constraints just like a control engineer creates control laws and that these controls can be derived from the a point-wise optimal control problem. Using this understanding of motor control, we have developed a coherent framework for the derivation of control laws for a variety of different control problems ranging from task-space control to hierarchical control. We have shown that this framework can be used in order to unify a variety of previous control approaches. We discussed the necessary conditions for both task-space and joint-space stability in this framework. Evaluations for an anthropomorphic robot arm of the framework in the area of operational space control are presented.

In Chapter 3, we have presented a framework for learning operational space control based upon the insights presented in Chapter 2. We first showed how small modeling errors as they always occur in practice can affect our ability to apply analytically derived operational space laws and, thus, that it is necessary to learn operational control laws. Our previous insight (i.e., that we have a point-wise optimal control problem) allowed us to reformulate the resulting learning problem as an immediate reward reinforcement learning problem. For this reason, we derived an immediate reward reinforcement learning algorithm based upon the expectation-maximization algorithm. The usage of normally distributed exploration allowed the derivation of a reward-weighted regression algorithm. The function approximation for representing the nominal behaviour of the policy was determined using a multiple paired inverse-forward models approach. This algorithm is applied to both a simulated three degrees of freedom robot arm and a simulated anthropomorphic SARCOS Master Arm. For the three degrees of freedom robot arm, we can show convergence to the optimal solution which can be determined analytically and for the simulated anthropomorphic SARCOS Master Arm, we can show very good tracking performance with high rewards.

In Chapter 4, we have presented the most extensive review of policy gradient methods to date as well as novel approaches. We started out by introducing the two general approaches for policy gradients in the machine learning literature, i.e., finite-difference gradients and likelihood ratio policy gradients, i.e., 'vanilla' policy gradients. We have derived both G(PO)MDP as well as the policy gradient theorem from the episodic point of view on likelihood ratio policy gradients. We have shown how to derive the optimal baselines for such estimators. Subsequently, we introduce the compatible function approximation which allows variance reduction but does not introduce bias into into the gradient approximation. We have clarified the discussion of the compatible function approximation and show that in general, it can only present the advantage function. The path-based derivation allows us find the natural policy gradient, i.e., the steepest descent for the path-based Fisher information matrix. Using this path-based derivation, we have proven Kakade's intuitive assumption that the parameters of the compatible function approximation are in fact the natural policy gradient. Using additional basis functions, we made use of both the compatible function approximation and the natural policy gradient in order to present a new reinforcement learning architecture, the Natural Actor-Critic. We show three resulting algorithms, i.e., the Natural Actor-Critic with general basis functions which employs LSTD-Q(λ) for gradient estimation and the episodic versions which do not require complex additional function approximation but only a constant parameter or time-variant parameter. We have shown that the natural policy gradient used in this book is in fact covariant. We have derived previous reinforcement learning methods such as the original Actor-Critic and the Bradke's LQR Q-Learning from the Natural Actor-Critic. Most presented algorithms are compared in the setting of motor primitive optimization where the episodic Natural Actor-Critic algorithms outperform previous approaches by orders of magnitude. The applicability to robotics is presented in a T-Ball hitting example where the SARCOS Master Arm has to hit a ball on a stand in a proper fashion.

In Summary, in this book, we have presented

- A general framework for control which serves as theoretical foundation and allows the unification of many previous control approaches (Chapter 2).
- The first learning approach to operational space control to date (Chapter 3).
- The reward-weighted regression approach for immediate reinforcement learning (Chapter 3).
- A unified treatment of previous policy gradient reinforcement learning approaches from the path-based perspective and their application to motor primitives (Chapter 4).
- With the Natural Actor-Critic, we have introduced a novel reinforcement learning method which is currently considered the **"method of choice"** (Aberdeen, 2006) in policy gradient methods and works well in the context of motor skill improvement in a T-Ball setup (Chapter 4).

These contributions together form the basis for motor skill learning in robotics.

5.2 Discussion: The Next Steps for Skill Learning

While this book has made important contributions to the domain of motor skill learning, it mainly delivers the building blocks required in order to create truly autonomous system, such (i) a general framework as foundation, (ii) a learning framework for motor command generation for execution in task space and (iii) a task learning framework based on policy gradients and motor primitives. At this point, we understand these three areas sufficiently well in order to discuss the required next steps for motor skill learning which are the collection of skills into libraries, the learning of skill selection as well as the sequencing and parallelization of motor primitives.

Skill Libraries. In Chapter 4, we have discussed how single behaviours in a certain task-space can be learned using parameterized motor primitives and in Chapter 3 we have discussed how to learn the execution of a motor task in its appropriate operational space. It is quite clear, that humans operate in multiple task spaces depending on the accomplished motor skill, e.g., in body-centric or retinal coordinates (Boussaoud & Bremmer, 1999). However, it appears that the motor primitives used by a human being for hand-writing or hand-zig-zagging are exactly the same as used for performing the task with a toe (Wing, 2000). Thus, the motor primitive programs seem to be kinematic plans in task-space, largely independent from the motor command generation. Thus, future skill libraries will contain both motor primitives as well as task-space to motor command transformations in order to make many combinations of the two possible. However, the learning of such skills will be largely using the methods presented in this book. It will use the observed movements in order to learn "coordinate system to motor command transformations", even if the performed task was in a different coordinate system. Separately from the task primitive to motor command transformation, we will learn motor primitives. For this, observed tasks are compared to existing primitives. If the observed task is equivalent to an existing one, it will be used for refining the primitive while otherwise it will it will be added to the skill library. Subsequently, the skill library manager needs to decide whether to practice the skill using the reinforcement learning methods presented in this book.

Learning to Select Skills. The selection of skills shifts the focus away from pure motor control towards a perceptuo-motor perspective. In this case, a general task is given, e.g., grasp a specified object and pick it up, move through the room along a global trajectory, or hit a ball with a tennis racket. Here, perceptual variables allow us to choose the right motor primitives, e.g., whether to select a power grasp vs a precision pinch for a particular object, which foot trajectories to use for moving from one foothold to another in the presence of obstacles, or whether to select a tennis fore- vs backhand. Similarly, they need to be used in order to set the motor primitive goal parameters, e.g., the contact points where we intend to hold the object, the selected next foothold, or where to hit the ball at what time. Each of these tasks is associated with the appropriate effector. However, it is quite obvious that some of the tasks do transfer between end-effectors, e.g., we could use two fingers or two hands for generating a precision pinch for grasping and lifting a particular object.

Clearly, the next higher system above the skill selection system needs some form of higher-level intelligence which determines the general task. This layer could close the gap between artificial intelligence systems and robotics.

Motor Primitive Sequencing and Parallelization. Another key issue for future research is the parallelization and sequencing of motor primitives. Such issues will automatically arise in tasks of higher complexity, e.g., assembling a modular system such as an IKEA shelf. For such tasks, we require a sequence of tasks such as first several a peg-in-the-hole tasks (Gullapalli et al., 1994) and subsequently dropping a shelf on top of the four pegs. It will also require holding two sides of the shelf in parallel so that they do not fall before assembled together. In order to learn such tasks, we require a hybrid control architecture consisting out of the lower level components such as motor primitives and task execution as well as a higher, discrete layer. The state of this discrete layer are the active primitives which together form a macro state or option. Such approaches will require a fusion of previous approaches to hybrid control approaches, hierarchical reinforcement learning and imitation learning similar as discussed in (Peters, 2005). Working towards such complex task compositions is of essential importance for the future of motor skills in robotics.

References

Aberdeen, D. (2006). POMDPs and policy gradients. In *Proceedings of the Machine Learning Summer School (MLSS)*. Canberra, Australia.

Aleksandrov, V., Sysoyev, V., & Shemeneva, V. (1968). Stochastic optimization. *Engineering Cybernetics*, *5*, 11–16.

Amari, S. (1998). Natural gradient works efficiently in learning. *Neural Computation*, *10*(251).

An, C. H., Atkeson, C. G., & Hollerbach, J. M. (1988). *Model-based control of a robot manipulator.* Cambridge, MA: MIT Press.

Arimoto, S. (1996). *Control theory of nonlinear mechanical systems: A passivity-based and circuit-theoretic approach.* Oxford, UK: Oxford University Press.

Atkeson, C. G. (1994). Using local trajectory optimizers to speed up global optimization in dynamic programming. In J. E. H. S. J. Moody & R. P. Lippmann (Eds.), *Advances in Neural Information Processing Systems 6* (pp. 503–521). Morgan Kaufmann.

Bagnell, J., & Schneider, J. (2003). Covariant policy search. In *Proceedings of the International Joint Conference on Artificial Intelligence (IJCAI)*. Acapulco, Mexico.

Baillieul, J., & Martin, D. P. (1990). Resolution of kinematic redundancy. In *Proceedings of Symposia in Applied Mathematics* (Vol. 41, pp. 49–89). San Diego, May 1990: Providence, RI: American Mathematical Society.

Baird, L. (1993). *Advantage updating* (Technical Report No. WL-TR-93-1146). Wright-Patterson Air Force Base, OH: Wright Laboratory.

Balasubramanian, V. (1997). Statistical inference, occam's razor, and statistical mechanics on the space of probability distributions. *Neural Computation*, *9*(2), 349-368.

Bartlett, P. (2002). An introduction to reinforcement learning theory: Value function methods. In *Proceedings of the Machine Learning Summer School (MLSS)* (p. 184-202). Canberra, Australia.

Baxter, J., & Bartlett, P. (2001). Infinite-horizon policy-gradient estimation. *Journal of Artificial Intelligence Research, 15*, 319-350.

Baxter, J., Bartlett, P., & Weaver, L. (2001). Experiments with infinite-horizon, policy-gradient estimation. *Journal of Artificial Intelligence Research, 15*, 351-381.

Beard, R., & McLain, T. (1998). Successive Galerkin approximation algorithms for nonlinear optimal and robust control. *International Journal of Control: Special Issue on Breakthroughs in the Control of Nonlinear Systems, 71*(5), 717–743.

Benbrahim, H., Doleac, J., Franklin, J., & Selfridge, O. (1992). Real-time learning: A ball on a beam. In *Proceedings of the International Joint Conference on Neural Networks (IJCNN)*. Baltimore, MD.

Benbrahim, H., & Franklin, J. (1997). Biped dynamic walking using reinforcement learning. *Robotics and Autonomous Systems, 22*, 283–302.

Berny, A. (2000). Statistical machine learning and combinatorial optimization. In L. Kallel, B. Naudts, & A. Rogers (Eds.), *Theoretical aspects of evolutionary computing* (Vol. 1). Heidelberg, Germany: Springer-Verlag.

Boussaoud, D., & Bremmer, F. (1999). Gaze effects in the cerebral cortex: Reference frames for space coding and action. *Exp Brain Res, 128*, 170–180.

Boyan, J. (1999). Least-squares temporal difference learning. In *Proceedings of the International Conference on Machine Learning (ICML)* (pp. 49–56). Bled, Slovenia.

Bradtke, S., Ydstie, E., & Barto, A. (1994). *Adaptive linear quadratic control using policy iteration* (Technical report No. UM-CS-1994-049). Amherst, MA: University of Massachusetts.

Bruyninckx, H., & Khatib, O. (2000). Gauss' principle and the dynamics of redundant and constrained manipulators. In *Proceedings of IEEE International Conference on Robotics and Automation (ICRA)* (pp. 2563–2569). San Francisco, CA.

Bullo, F., & Lewis, A. D. (2004). *Geometric control of mechanical systems modeling, analysis, and design for simple mechanical control systems*. Heidelberg, Germany: Springer-Verlag.

Bullock, D., Grossberg, S., & Guenther, F. H. (1993). A self-organizing neural model of motor equivalent reaching and tool use by a multijoint arm. *Journal of Cognitive Neuroscience, 5*(4), 408–435.

Chung, W., Chung, W., & Y.Youm. (1993). Null torque based dynamic control for kinematically redundant manipulators. *Journal of Robotic Systems, 10*(6), 811–834.

Craig, J. (2005). *Introduction to Robotics: Mechanics and Control.* Upper Saddle River, NJ: Pearson Prentice Hall.

Dayan, P., & Hinton, G. E. (1997). Using expectation-maximization for reinforcement learning. *Neural Computation, 9*(2), 271-278.

De Wit, C., Siciliano, B., & Bastin, G. (1996). *Theory of robot control.* Heidelberg, Germany: Springer-Verlag.

De Luca, A., & Mataloni, F. (1991). Learning control for redundant manipulators. In *Proceedings of IEEE International Conference on Robotics and Automation (ICRA).* Sacramento, CA.

Doty, K., Melchiorri, C., & Bonivento, C. (1993). A theory of generalized inverses applied to robotics. *International Journal of Robotics Research, 12*, 1–19.

D'Souza, A., Vijayakumar, S., & Schaal, S. (2001). Learning inverse kinematics. In *Proceedings of the IEEE/RSJ International Conference on Intelligent Robots and Systems (IROS).* Hawaii, USA.

Dyer, P., & McReynolds, S. R. (1970). *The computation and theory of optimal control.* New York, NY: Academic Press.

Endo, G., Morimoto, J., Matsubara, T., Nakanishi, J., & Cheng, G. (2005). Learning cpg sensory feedback with policy gradient for biped locomotion for a full-body humanoid. In *Proceedings of the National Conference on Artificial Intelligence (AAAI).* Pittsburgh, PA.

Fletcher, R., & Fletcher, R. (2000). *Practical methods of optimization.* New York, NY: John Wiley & Sons.

Glynn, P. (1987). Likelihood ratio gradient estimation: an overview. In *Proceedings of the Winter Simulation Conference (WSC)* (p. 366-375). Atlanta, GA.

Glynn, P. (1990). Likelihood ratio gradient estimation for stochastic systems. *Communications of the ACM, 33*(10), 75–84.

Greensmith, E., Bartlett, P., & Baxter, J. (2001). Variance reduction techniques for gradient estimates in reinforcement learning. *Advances in Neural Information Processing Systems, 14*(34).

Greensmith, E., Bartlett, P. L., & Baxter, J. (2004). Variance reduction techniques for gradient estimates in reinforcement learning. *Journal of Machine Learning Research, 5*, 1471–1530.

Guenter, F., Hersch, M., Calinon, S., & Billard, A. (2007). Reinforcement learning for imitating constrained reaching movements. *Advanced Robotics, In Press.*

Guez, A., & Ahmad, Z. (1988). Solution to the inverse kinematics problem in robotics by neural networks. In *Proceedings of IEEE International Conference on Neural Networks* (pp. 102–108). San Diego, CA.

Gullapalli, V. (1991). Associative reinforcement learning of real-value functions. In *Proceedings of the IEEE International Conference on Systems, Man and Cybernetics.* Charlottesville, VA.

Gullapalli, V., Franklin, J., & Benbrahim, H. (1994). Aquiring robot skills via reinforcement learning. *IEEE Control Systems Journal, Special Issue on Robotics: Capturing Natural Motion*, *4*(1), 13-24.

Hanafusa, H., Yoshikawa, T., & Nakamura, Y. (1981). Analysis and control of articulated robot with redundancy. In *Proceedings of IFAC Symposium on Robot Control* (Vol. 4, pp. 1927–1932). Gaithersburg, MD.

Haruno, M., Wolpert, D. M., & Kawato, M. (1999). Multiple paired forward-inverse models for human motor learning and control. In *Advances in Neural Information Processing Systems.* Cambridge, MA: MIT Press.

Harville, D. A. (2000). *Matrix algebra from a statistician's perspective.* Heidelberg, Germany: Springer Verlag.

Hasdorff, L. (1976). *Gradient optimization and nonlinear control.* New York, NY: John Wiley & Sons.

Hirzinger, G., Sporer, N., Albu-Schäffer, A., Hähnle, M., Krenn, R., Pascucci, A., & Schedl, M. (2002). DLR's torque-controlled light weight robot III - are we reaching the technological limits now? In *Proceedings of IEEE International Conference on Robotics and Automation (ICRA)* (p. 1710-1716). Washington DC.

Hollerbach, J. M., & Suh, K. C. (1987). Redundancy resolution of manipulators through torque optimization. *International Journal of Robotics and Automation*, *3*(4), 308–316.

Hsu, P., Hauser, J., & Sastry, S. (1989). Dynamic control of redundant manipulators. *Journal of Robotic Systems*, *6*(2), 133–148.

Ijspeert, A., Nakanishi, J., & Schaal, S. (2003). Learning attractor landscapes for learning motor primitives. In S. Becker, S. Thrun, & K. Obermayer (Eds.), *Advances in Neural Information Processing Systems* (Vol. 15, pp. 1547–1554). Cambridge, MA: MIT Press.

Ijspeert, J. A., Nakanishi, J., & Schaal, S. (2002). Movement imitation with nonlinear dynamical systems in humanoid robots. In *Proceedings of IEEE International Conference on Robotics and Automation (ICRA).* Washinton, DC.

Isidori, A. (1995). *Nonlinear control systems.* Heidelberg, Germany: Springer-Verlag.

Jacobson, D. H., & Mayne, D. Q. (1970). *Differential dynamic programming.* New York, NY: American Elsevier Publishing Company, Inc.

Jordan, I. M., & Rumelhart. (1992). Supervised learning with a distal teacher. *Cognitive Science, 16*, 307–354.

Kaebling, L. P., Littman, M. L., & Moore, A. W. (1996). Reinforcement learning: A survey. *Journal of Artificial Intelligence Research, 4*, 237–285.

Kakade, S. (2001). Optimizing average reward using discounted rewards. In *Proceedings of the Conference on Computational Learning Theory (COLT).* Amsterdam, Netherlands.

Kakade, S. A. (2002). Natural policy gradient. In *Advances in Neural Information Processing Systems* (Vol. 14). Vancouver, CA.

Kazerounian, K., & Wang, Z. (1988). Global versus local optimization in redundancy resolution of robotic manipulators. *International Journal of Robotics Research, 7*(5), 3-12.

K.C.Suh, & Hollerbach, J. M. (1987). Local versus global torque optimization of redundant manipulators. In *Proceedings of the International Conference on Robotics and Automation (ICRA)* (pp. 619–624). Raleigh, NC.

Khatib, O. (1987). A unified approach for motion and force control of robot manipulators: The operational space formulation. *IEEE Journal of Robotics and Automation, 3*(1), 43–53.

Khatib, O., Sentis, L., Park, J., & Warren, J. (2004). Whole body dynamic behavior and control of human-like robots. *International Journal of Humanoid Robotics, 1*(1), 29–43.

Kimura, H., & Kobayashi, S. (1997). Reinforcement learning for locomotion of a two-linked robot arm. In *Proceedings of the Europian Workshop on Learning Robots (EWLR)* (pp. 144–153). Brighton, UK.

Kimura, H., & Kobayashi, S. (1998). Reinforcement learning for continuous action using stochastic gradient ascent. In *Proceedings of the International Conference on Intelligent Autonomous Systems (IAS)* (Vol. 5, pp. 288–295). Madison, Wisconsin.

Kleinman, N., Spall, J., & Naiman, D. (1999). Simulation-based optimization with stochastic approximation using common random numbers,". *Management Science, 45*, 1570–1578.

Kohl, N., & Stone, P. (2004). Policy gradient reinforcement learning for fast quadrupedal locomotion. In *Proceedings of the IEEE International Conference on Robotics and Automation (ICRA)*. New Orleans, LA.

Konda, V., & Tsitsiklis, J. (2000). Actor-critic algorithms. *Advances in Neural Information Processing Systems 12*.

Lawrence, G., Cowan, N., & Russell, S. (2003). Efficient gradient estimation for motor control learning. In *Proceedings of the International Conference on Uncertainty in Artificial Intelligence (UAI)*. Acapulco, Mexico.

Maciejewski, A., & Klein, C. (1985). Obstacle avoidance for kinematically redundant manipulators in dynamically varying environments. *International Journal of Robotics Research*, *4*(3), 109–117.

Minamide, N., & Nakamura, K. (1969). *Minimum error control problem in banach space* (Research Report of Automatic Control Lab No. 16). Nagoya, Japan: Nagoya University.

Mitsunaga, N., Smith, C., Kanda, T., Ishiguro, H., & Hagita, N. (2005). Robot behavior adaptation for human-robot interaction based on policy gradient reinforcement learning. In *Proceedings of the IEEE/RSJ International Conference on Intelligent Robots and Systems (IROS)* (p. 1594-1601). Edmonton, Canada.

Miyamoto, H., Gandolfo, F., Gomi, H., Schaal, S., Koike, Y., Osu, R., Nakano, E., & Kawato, M. (1995). A kendama learning robot based on a dynamic optimization theory. In *Proceedings of the IEEE International Workshop on Robot and Human Communication (ROMAN)* (pp. 327–332). Tokyo, Japan.

Miyamoto, H., Gandolfo, F., Gomi, H., Schaal, S., Koike, Y., Rieka, O., Nakano, E., Wada, Y., & Kawato, M. (1996). A kendama learning robot based on a dynamic optimization principle. In *Proceedings of the International Conference on Neural Information Processing (ICONIP)* (pp. 938–942). Hong Kong.

Moon, T., & Stirling, W. (2000). *Mathematical methods and algorithms for signal processing*. Upper Saddle River, NJ: Prentice Hall.

Mori, T., Nakamura, Y., & Ishii, S. (2005). Efficient sample reuse by off-policy natural actor-critic learning. In *Advances in Neural Information Processing Systems (NIPS '05 Workshop)*. Vancouver, Canada.

Mori, T., Nakamura, Y., Sato, M. aki, & Ishii, S. (2004). Reinforcement learning for cpg-driven biped robot. In *Proceedings of the National Conference on Artificial Intelligence (AAAI)* (p. 623-630). San Jose, CA.

Morimoto, J., & Atkeson, C. A. (2003). Minimax differential dynamic programming: an application to robust biped walking. In S. Becker, S. Thrun, & K. Obermayer (Eds.), *Advances in Neural Information Processing Systems 15.* Cambridge, MA: MIT Press.

Nakamura, Y. (1991). *Advanced robotics: Redundancy and optimization.* Boston, MA: Addison-Wesley.

Nakamura, Y., Hanafusa, H., & Yoshikawa, T. (1987). Task-priority based control of robot manipulators. *International Journal of Robotics Research, 6*(2), 3–15.

Nakamura, Y., Mori, T., & Ishii, S. (2004). Natural policy gradient reinforcement learning for a cpg control of a biped robot. In *Proceedings of the International Conference on Parallel Problem Solving from Nature (PPSN)* (p. 972-981). Kyoto, Japan.

Nakanishi, J., Cory, R., Mistry, M., Peters, J., & Schaal, S. (2005). Comparative experiments on task space control with redundancy resolution. In *Proceedings of the IEEE/RSJ International Conference on Intelligent Robots and Systems (IROS).* Edmonton, Canada.

Nakanishi, J., Farrell, J. A., & Schaal, S. (2004). Learning composite adaptive control for a class of nonlinear systems. In *Proceedings of the International Conference on Robotics and Automation (ICRA)* (pp. 2647–2652). New Orleans, LA.

Ng, A. Y., & Jordan, M. (2000). PEGASUS: A policy search method for large MDPs and POMDPs. In *Proceedings of the International Conference on Uncertainty in Artificial Intelligence (UAI).* Palo Alto, CA.

Park, J., Chung, W.-K., & Youm, Y. (1995). Specification and control of motion for kinematically redundant manipulators. In *Proceedings of the IEEE/RSJ International Conference on Intelligent Robots and Systems (IROS).* Las Vegas, USA.

Park, J., Chung, W.-K., & Youm, Y. (2002). Characterization of instability of dynamic control for kinematically redundant manipulators. In *Proceedings of the International Conference on Robotics and Automation (ICRA).* Washington, DC.

Park, J., Kim, J., & Kang, D. (2005). An RLS-Based Natural Actor-Critic Algorithm for Locomotion of a Two-Linked Robot Arm. In Y. Hao, J. Liu, Y. Wang, Y. ming Cheung, H. Yin, L. Jiao, J. Ma, & Y.-C. Jiao (Eds.), *Proceedings of the International Conference on Computational Intelligence and Security (CIS)* (Vol. 3801, pp. 65–72). Xi'an, China: Springer.

Peters, J. (2005). *Machine learning of motor skills for robotics* (Technical Report No. CS-05-867). Los Angeles, CA: University of Southern California.

Peters, J., Mistry, M., Udwadia, F., R.Cory, Nakanishi, J., & Schaal, S. (2005). A unifying methodology for the control of robotic systems. In *Proceedings of the IEEE/RSJ International Conference on Intelligent Robots and Systems (IROS)*. Edmonton, Canada.

Peters, J., Mistry, M., Udwadia, F. E., & Schaal, S. (2005). A new methodology for robot control design. In *ASME International Conference on Multibody Systems, Nonlinear Dynamics, and Control (MSNDC 2005)*. Long Beach, CA.

Peters, J., & Schaal, S. (2006a). Learning operational space control. In *Proceedings of Robotics: Science and Systems (RSS)*. Philadelphia, PA.

Peters, J., & Schaal, S. (2006b). Policy gradient methods for robotics. In *Proceedings of the IEEE/RSJ International Conference on Intelligent Robots and Systems (IROS)*. Beijing, China.

Peters, J., & Schaal, S. (2007a). Reinforcement learning for operational space. In *Proceedings of the International Conference on Robotics and Automation (ICRA)*. Rome, Italy.

Peters, J., & Schaal, S. (2007b). Using reward-weighted regression for reinforcement learning of task space control. In *Proceedings of the IEEE International Symposium on Approximate Dynamic Programming and Reinforcement Learning (ADPRL)*. Honolulu, HI.

Peters, J., Vijayakumar, S., & Schaal, S. (2003a). Reinforcement learning for humanoid robotics. In *Proceedings of the IEEE-RAS International Conference on Humanoid Robots (HUMANOIDS)*. Karlsruhe, Germany.

Peters, J., Vijayakumar, S., & Schaal, S. (2003b). Scaling reinforcement learning paradigms for motor learning. In *Proceedings of the 10th Joint Symposium on Neural Computation (JSNC)*. Irvine, CA.

Peters, J., Vijayakumar, S., & Schaal, S. (2005). Natural actor-critic. In *Proceedings of the European Machine Learning Conference (ECML)*. Porto, Portugal.

Pratt, J., & Pratt, G. (1998). Intuitive control of a planar bipedal walking robot. In *Proceedings of the International Conference on Robotics and Automation (ICRA)* (pp. 1024–2021). Leuven, Belgium.

Richter, S., Aberdeen, D., & Yu, J. (2007). Natural actor-critic for road traffic optimisation. In B. Schoelkopf, J. Platt, & T. Hofmann (Eds.), *Advances in Neural Information Processing Systems* (Vol. 19). Cambridge, MA: MIT Press.

Sadegh, P., & Spall, J. (1997). Optimal random perturbations for stochastic approximation using a simultaneous perturbation gradient approximation. In *Proceedings of the American Control Conference (ACC)* (p. 3582-3586). Albuquerque, NM.

Samson, C., Borgne, M. L., & Espiau, B. (1991). *Robot Control: The Task Function Approach.* Oxford, UK: Oxford University Press.

Sato, M., Nakamura, Y., & Ishii, S. (2002). Reinforcement learning for biped locomotion. In *Proceedings of the International Conference on Artificial Neural Networks (ICANN)* (p. 777-782). Springer-Verlag.

Schaal, S., Atkeson, C. G., & Vijayakumar, S. (2002). Scalable techniques from nonparameteric statistics for real-time robot learning. *Applied Intelligence, 17*(1), 49–60.

Schaal, S., Ijspeert, A., & Billard, A. (2004). Computational approaches to motor learning by imitation. In C. D. Frith & D. Wolpert (Eds.), *The neuroscience of social interaction* (pp. 199–218). Oxford, UK: Oxford University Press.

Sciavicco, L., & Siciliano, B. (2007). *Modeling and control of robot manipulators.* Heidelberg, Germany: MacGraw-Hill.

Sentis, L., & Khatib, O. (2004). A prioritized multi-objective dynamic controller for robots in human environments. In *Proceedings of the IEEE-RAS International Conference on Humanoid Robots (HUMANOIDS).* Los Angeles, USA.

Sentis, L., & Khatib, O. (2005). Control of free-floating humanoid robots through task prioritization. In *Proceedings of the International Conference on Robotics and Automation (ICRA).* Barcelona, Spain.

Siciliano, B., & Slotine, J. (1991). A general framework for managing multiple tasks in highly redundant robotic systems. In *Proceedings of the International Conference on Robotics and Automation (ICRA)* (pp. 1211–1216). Pisa, Italy.

Spall, J. C. (2003). *Introduction to stochastic search and optimization: Estimation, simulation, and control.* Hoboken, NJ: Wiley.

Spong, M., Thorp, J., & Kleinwaks, J. (1984). On pointwise optimal control strategies for robot manipulators. In *Proceedings of the Annual Conference on Information Sciences and Systems.* Princeton, NJ.

Spong, M., Thorp, J., & Kleinwaks, J. (1986). The control of robot manipulators with bounded input. *IEEE Transactions on Automatic Control, 31*(6), 483-490.

Su, F., & Gibbs, A. (2002). On choosing and bounding probability metrics. *International Statistical Review, 70*(3), 419-435.

Sutton, R., & Barto, A. (1998). *Reinforcement learning.* Boston, MA: MIT Press.

Sutton, R. S., McAllester, D., Singh, S., & Mansour, Y. (2000). Policy gradient methods for reinforcement learning with function approximation. In S. A. Solla, T. K. Leen, & K.-R. Mueller (Eds.), *Advances in Neural Information Processing Systems (NIPS).* Denver, CO: MIT Press.

Tedrake, R., Zhang, T. W., & Seung, H. S. (2005). Learning to walk in 20 minutes. In *Proceedings of the Yale Workshop on Adaptive and Learning Systems.* New Haven, CT: Yale University, New Haven.

Tevatia, G., & Schaal, S. (2000). Inverse kinematics for humanoid robots. In *Proceedings of the International Conference on Robotics and Automation (ICRA).* San Fransisco, CA.

Tsai, L.-W. (1999). *Robot analysis.* New York, NY: Wiley.

Udwadia, F. E. (2003). A new perspective on tracking control of nonlinear structural and mechanical systems. *Proceedings of the Royal Society of London, Series A, 2003*(439), 1783–1800.

Udwadia, F. E. (2005). *Discussions on C.F. Gauss, Gauss' principle, and its application to control.* (Personal communication)

Udwadia, F. E., & Kalaba, R. E. (1996). *Analytical dynamics: A new approach.* Cambridge, UK: Cambridge University Press.

Ueno, T., Nakamura, Y., Takuma, T., Shibata, T., Hosoda, K., & Ishii, S. (2006). Fast and stable learning of quasi-passive dynamic walking by an unstable biped robot based on off-policy natural actor-critic. In *Proceedings of the IEEE/RSJ International Conference on Intelligent Robots and Systems (IROS).* Beijing, China.

Vachenauer, P., Rade, L., & Westergren, B. (2000). *Springers Mathematische Formeln: Taschenbuch für Ingenieure, Naturwissenschaftler, Informatiker, Wirtschaftswissenschaftler.* Heidelberg, Germany: Springer-Verlag.

Wahba, G., & Nashed, M. Z. (1973). The approximate solution of a class of constrained control problems. In *Proceedings of the Sixth Hawaii International Conference on Systems Sciences.* Hawaii, HI.

Weaver, L., & Tao, N. (2001a). The optimal reward baseline for gradient-based reinforcement learning. In *Proceedings of the International Conference on Uncertainty in Artificial Intelligence (UAI)* (Vol. 17). Seattle, Washington.

Weaver, L., & Tao, N. (2001b). *The variance minimizing constant reward baseline for gradient-based reinforcement learning* (Technical Report No. 30). Australian National University (ANU).

Werbos, P. (1979). Changes in global policy analysis procedures suggested by new methods of optimization. *Policy Analysis and Information Systems, 3*(1).

Williams, R. J. (1992). Simple statistical gradient-following algorithms for connectionist reinforcement learning. *Machine Learning, 8*(23).

Wing, A. M. (2000). Motor control: Mechanisms of motor equivalence in handwriting. *Current Biology*, *10*(6), 245–248.

Yamane, K., & Nakamura, Y. (2003). Natural motion animation through constraining and deconstraining at will constraining and deconstraining at will. *IEEE Transaction on Visualization and Computer Graphics*, *9*(3).

Yoshikawa, T. (1990). *Foundations of Robotics: Analysis and Control.* Boston, MA: MIT Press.

Appendix A

Additional Derivations and Discussion

A.1 Steepest Descent with Respect to a Metric N

In this section, we show how to determine the steepest decent with respect to a metric and prove the results from Section 4.4.1. We have the optimization problem

$$\max J(\boldsymbol{\theta} + \boldsymbol{\delta\theta}) = J(\boldsymbol{\theta}) + \boldsymbol{\nabla} J(\boldsymbol{\theta})^T \boldsymbol{\delta\theta},$$
$$s.t. d(\boldsymbol{\theta} + \boldsymbol{\delta\theta}, \boldsymbol{\theta}) = \frac{1}{2}\boldsymbol{\delta\theta}^T \mathrm{N} \boldsymbol{\delta\theta} = \varepsilon.$$

Thus, we have the Langrangian

$$L(\boldsymbol{\delta\theta}, \lambda) = J(\boldsymbol{\theta}) + \boldsymbol{\nabla} J(\boldsymbol{\theta})^T \boldsymbol{\delta\theta} + \lambda\left(\varepsilon - \frac{1}{2}\boldsymbol{\delta\theta}^T \mathrm{N} \boldsymbol{\delta\theta}\right)$$

which can be maximized with respect to $\boldsymbol{\delta\theta}$ which yields $\boldsymbol{\delta\theta} = \lambda^{-1}\mathrm{N}^{-1}\boldsymbol{\nabla} J(\boldsymbol{\theta})$. Then we have the dual function

$$g(\lambda) = J(\boldsymbol{\theta}) + \frac{1}{2}\lambda^{-1}\boldsymbol{\nabla} J(\boldsymbol{\theta})^T \mathrm{N}^{-1}\boldsymbol{\nabla} J(\boldsymbol{\theta}) + \lambda\varepsilon$$

which gives us the Langrangian multiplier

$$\lambda = \sqrt{\frac{\boldsymbol{\nabla} J(\boldsymbol{\theta})^T \mathrm{N}^{-1}\boldsymbol{\nabla} J(\boldsymbol{\theta})}{\varepsilon}}.$$

Therefore, we have the steepest gradient descent of $\boldsymbol{\theta}_{n+1} = \boldsymbol{\theta}_n + \alpha_n \mathrm{N}^{-1}\boldsymbol{\nabla} J(\boldsymbol{\theta})$ with a learning rate

$$\alpha_n = \lambda^{-1} = \sqrt{\frac{\varepsilon}{\boldsymbol{\nabla} J(\boldsymbol{\theta})^T \mathrm{N}^{-1}\boldsymbol{\nabla} J(\boldsymbol{\theta})}}.$$

The learning rate α_n is not necessarily a desirable one and can be replaced by a constant learning rate without changing the gradients direction.

A.2 Proof of the Covariance Theorem

For small parameter changes $\Delta\mathbf{h}$ and $\Delta\boldsymbol{\theta}$, we have $\Delta\boldsymbol{\theta} = \nabla_{\mathbf{h}}\boldsymbol{\theta}^T\Delta\mathbf{h}$. If the natural policy gradient is a covariant update rule, a change $\Delta\mathbf{h}$ along the gradient $\nabla_{\mathbf{h}}J(\mathbf{h})$ would result in the same change $\Delta\boldsymbol{\theta}$ along the gradient $\nabla_{\boldsymbol{\theta}}J(\boldsymbol{\theta})$ for the same scalar step-size α. By differentiation, we can obtain $\nabla_{\mathbf{h}}J(\mathbf{h}) = \nabla_{\mathbf{h}}\boldsymbol{\theta}\nabla_{\boldsymbol{\theta}}J(\boldsymbol{\theta})$.It is straightforward to show that the Fisher information matrix includes the Jacobian $\nabla_{\mathbf{h}}\boldsymbol{\theta}$ twice as factor,

$$\begin{aligned}\mathbf{F}(\mathbf{h}) &= \int_{\mathbb{X}} d^{\pi}(\mathbf{x}) \int_{\mathbb{U}} \pi(\mathbf{u}|\mathbf{x})\nabla_{\mathbf{h}}\log\pi(\mathbf{u}|\mathbf{x})\nabla_{\mathbf{h}}\log\pi(\mathbf{u}|\mathbf{x})^T d\mathbf{u}d\mathbf{x},\\ &= \nabla_{\mathbf{h}}\boldsymbol{\theta}\int_{\mathbb{X}} d^{\pi}(\mathbf{x}) \int_{\mathbb{U}} \pi(\mathbf{u}|\mathbf{x})\nabla_{\boldsymbol{\theta}}\log\pi(\mathbf{u}|\mathbf{x})\nabla_{\boldsymbol{\theta}}\log\pi(\mathbf{u}|\mathbf{x})^T d\mathbf{u}d\mathbf{x}\nabla_{\mathbf{h}}\boldsymbol{\theta}^T,\\ &= \nabla_{\mathbf{h}}\boldsymbol{\theta}\mathbf{F}(\boldsymbol{\theta})\nabla_{\mathbf{h}}\boldsymbol{\theta}^T.\end{aligned}$$

This shows that natural gradient in the $\mathbf{h}$ parameterization is given by

$$\widetilde{\nabla}_{\mathbf{h}}J(\mathbf{h}) = \mathbf{F}^{-1}(\mathbf{h})\nabla_{\mathbf{h}}J(\mathbf{h}) = \left(\nabla_{\mathbf{h}}\boldsymbol{\theta}\mathbf{F}(\boldsymbol{\theta})\nabla_{\mathbf{h}}\boldsymbol{\theta}^T\right)^{-1}\nabla_{\mathbf{h}}\boldsymbol{\theta}\nabla_{\boldsymbol{\theta}}J(\boldsymbol{\theta}).$$

This has a surprising implication as it makes it straightforward to see that the natural policy is covariant since

$$\begin{aligned}\Delta\boldsymbol{\theta} &= \alpha\nabla_{\mathbf{h}}\boldsymbol{\theta}^T\Delta\mathbf{h} = \alpha\nabla_{\mathbf{h}}\boldsymbol{\theta}^T\widetilde{\nabla}_{\mathbf{h}}J(\mathbf{h}),\\ &= \alpha\nabla_{\mathbf{h}}\boldsymbol{\theta}^T\left(\nabla_{\mathbf{h}}\boldsymbol{\theta}\mathbf{F}(\boldsymbol{\theta})\nabla_{\mathbf{h}}\boldsymbol{\theta}^T\right)^{-1}\nabla_{\mathbf{h}}\boldsymbol{\theta}\nabla_{\boldsymbol{\theta}}J(\boldsymbol{\theta}),\\ &= \alpha\mathbf{F}^{-1}(\boldsymbol{\theta})\nabla_{\boldsymbol{\theta}}J(\boldsymbol{\theta}) = \alpha\widetilde{\nabla}_{\boldsymbol{\theta}}J(\boldsymbol{\theta}),\end{aligned}$$

assuming that $\nabla_{\mathbf{h}}\boldsymbol{\theta}$ is invertible. This concludes that the natural policy gradient is in fact a **covariant** gradient update rule.

A.3 A Discussion of Kimura & Kobayashi's Algorithm

Kimura & Kobayashi's (1998) introduced a non-episodic algorithm based on value function approximation and policy gradients. Here, we show that this algorithm is in fact at best a biased version of the policy gradient. For this, we first show what value function based gradient estimators can be derived from both the policy gradient theorem and GPOMDP. As discussed 4, the true gradient of the policy gradient theorem is

$$\nabla J = \int d^{\pi}(x) \int \pi(u|x)\nabla\log\pi(u|x)\left[Q^{\pi}(x,u) - b(x)\right] du dx. \qquad \text{(A.1)}$$

In this equation, we can make use of the relation $Q^{\pi}(x,u) - b(x) = E\{r(x,u) + V(x') - V(x)\}$, and derive a resulting algorithm

$$\begin{aligned} \Delta\theta &= \alpha \left\langle \nabla \log \pi (u|x) \left[Q^{\pi}(x,u) - b(x) \right] \right\rangle, && \text{(A.2)} \\ &\approx \alpha \left\langle \nabla \log \pi (u|x) \left[r(x,u) + V(x') - V(x) \right] \right\rangle. && \text{(A.3)} \end{aligned}$$

This algorithm is called SRV, see (Gullapalli, 1991), and represents a true gradient. Similarly, we could try to derive Kimura's algorithm from the GPOMDP formulation, where each action gets credit for all future actions. There, we have

$$\nabla J = \int d^{\pi}(x) \int \pi(u|x) \left(\nabla \log d^{\pi}(x) + \nabla \log \pi(u|x) \right) \left[r(x,u) - b(x) \right] du dx, \tag{A.4}$$

and using $d^{\pi}(x') = \int\int d^{\pi}(x)\, \pi(u|x)\, dudx$, we realize that

$$d^{\pi}(x') \nabla \log d^{\pi}(x') = \left\langle \nabla \log \pi(u|x) + \nabla \log d^{\pi}(x) \right\rangle. \tag{A.5}$$

As an algorithm, this yields

$$\begin{aligned} D(x') &= \nabla \log \pi (u|x) + D(x), && \text{(A.6)} \\ \Delta\theta &= \alpha \left\langle \left[\nabla \log \pi (u|x) + D(x) \right] \left[r(x,u) - b(x) \right] \right\rangle. && \text{(A.7)} \end{aligned}$$

Again, this Episodic REINFORCE and represents a true gradient but not Kimura's algorithm! If we use a forgetting factor in $D(x') = \nabla \log \pi(u|x) + \beta D(x)$ as suggested in (Baxter & Bartlett, 2001), it will introduce a large bias, i.e., the optimal solution is altered! In LQR problems with $Q = 0.1$ and $A = B = R = 1$, a $\beta \approx 0.98$ will result in instable LQR solutions even if computed analytically.

Kimura & Kobayashi (1998) propose an algorithm which basically fuses the two correct algorithms into a single, biased policy gradient estimator

$$\begin{aligned} D(x') &= \nabla \log \pi (u|x) + \beta D(x), && \text{(A.8)} \\ \Delta\theta &= \alpha \left\langle \left[\nabla \log \pi (u|x) + D(x) \right] \left[r(x,u) + V(x') - V(x) \right] \right\rangle. && \text{(A.9)} \end{aligned}$$

As you notice, this does not give you a true gradient as

$$\nabla J \neq \int d^{\pi}(x) \int \pi(u|x) \left(\nabla \log d^{\pi}(x) + \nabla \log \pi(u|x) \right) \left[Q^{\pi}(x,u) - b(x) \right] du dx. \tag{A.10}$$

Thus, we have a *biased gradient.* It will work for some cases but it is nothing but a heuristic which works accidentally.

A.4 Derivations of the Two Forms of the eNAC

In this section, we derive the two different forms of the Episodic Natural Actor-Critic in two different forms. For this, we first discuss a theorem needed for the derivation of estimators which simplifies the estimation of the compatible function approximation and subsequently apply it on the eNAC.

Theorem A.1 *A regression problem of the form*

$$\beta^* = \begin{bmatrix}\beta_1 & \beta_2\end{bmatrix}^T = \underset{\beta}{\operatorname{argmin}} \left(\mathbf{Y} - \mathbf{X}\beta\right)^T \left(\mathbf{Y} - \mathbf{X}\beta\right), \tag{A.11}$$

with basis function $\mathbf{X} = \begin{bmatrix}\mathbf{X}_1 & \mathbf{X}_2\end{bmatrix}$ *has the unique solution*

$$\beta_1 = \left(\mathbf{X}_1^T\mathbf{X}_1\right)^{-1} \mathbf{X}_1^T \left(\mathbf{Y} - \mathbf{X}_2\mathbf{b}\right), \tag{A.12}$$

$$\beta_2 = \mathbf{Q}^{-1}\mathbf{X}_2^T \left(\mathbf{Y} - \mathbf{X}_1 \left(\mathbf{X}_1^T\mathbf{X}_1\right)^{-1} \mathbf{X}_1^T\mathbf{Y}\right), \tag{A.13}$$

with

$$\begin{aligned}\mathbf{Q}^{-1} &= \left(\mathbf{X}_2^T\mathbf{X}_2\right)^{-1} \\ &+ \left(\mathbf{X}_2^T\mathbf{X}_2\right)^{-1} \mathbf{X}_2^T\mathbf{X}_1 \left(\mathbf{X}_1^T\mathbf{X}_1 - \mathbf{X}_1^T\mathbf{X}_2 \left(\mathbf{X}_2^T\mathbf{X}_2\right)^{-1} \mathbf{X}_2^T\mathbf{X}_1\right)^{-1} \mathbf{X}_1^T\mathbf{X}_2 \left(\mathbf{X}_2^T\mathbf{X}_2\right)^{-1}.\end{aligned} \tag{A.14}$$

Proof. The solution of the regression problem in Equation (A.11) is given by

$$\beta^* = \left(\mathbf{X}^T\mathbf{X}\right)^{-1} \mathbf{X}^T\mathbf{Y}, \tag{A.15}$$

see (Harville, 2000). By defining $\mathbf{T} = \mathbf{X}_1^T\mathbf{X}_1$, $\mathbf{U} = \mathbf{X}_1^T\mathbf{X}_2$, $\mathbf{W} = \mathbf{X}_2^T\mathbf{X}_2$, and subsequently applying the Matrix Inversion Theorem (see (Harville, 2000), pages 98–101), we obtain

$$\left(\mathbf{X}^T\mathbf{X}\right)^{-1} = \begin{bmatrix}\mathbf{T} & \mathbf{U} \\ \mathbf{U}^T & \mathbf{W}\end{bmatrix}^{-1} = \begin{bmatrix}\mathbf{T}^{-1} + \mathbf{T}^{-1}\mathbf{U}\mathbf{Q}^{-1}\mathbf{U}^T\mathbf{T}^{-1} & -\mathbf{T}^{-1}\mathbf{U}\mathbf{Q}^{-1} \\ -\mathbf{Q}^{-1}\mathbf{U}^T\mathbf{T}^{-1} & \mathbf{Q}^{-1}\end{bmatrix}, \tag{A.16}$$

with $\mathbf{Q} = \mathbf{W} - \mathbf{U}^T\mathbf{T}^{-1}\mathbf{U}$. We can simplify $\mathbf{Q}^{-1}$ using the Sherman-Morrison Theorem (see (Moon & Stirling, 2000), pages 258–259) which yields

$$\mathbf{Q}^{-1} = \mathbf{W}^{-1} + \mathbf{W}^{-1}\mathbf{U}^T \left(\mathbf{T} - \mathbf{U}\mathbf{W}^{-1}\mathbf{U}^T\right)^{-1} \mathbf{U}\mathbf{W}^{-1}. \tag{A.17}$$

When multiplying $\left(\mathbf{X}^T\mathbf{X}\right)^{-1}$ by $\mathbf{X}^T\mathbf{Y} = \begin{bmatrix}\mathbf{X}_1^T\mathbf{Y} & \mathbf{X}_2^T\mathbf{Y}\end{bmatrix}^T$, we obtain

$$\beta_1 = \left(\mathbf{T}^{-1} + \mathbf{T}^{-1}\mathbf{U}\mathbf{Q}^{-1}\mathbf{U}^T\mathbf{T}^{-1}\right) \mathbf{X}_1^T\mathbf{Y} - \mathbf{T}^{-1}\mathbf{U}\mathbf{Q}^{-1}\mathbf{X}_2^T\mathbf{Y}, \tag{A.18}$$

$$= \mathbf{T}^{-1} \left(\mathbf{X}_1^T\mathbf{Y} - \mathbf{U}\beta_2\right), \tag{A.19}$$

$$\beta_2 = \mathbf{Q}^{-1}\left(\mathbf{X}_2^T\mathbf{Y} - \mathbf{U}^T\mathbf{T}^{-1}\mathbf{X}_1^T\mathbf{Y}\right). \tag{A.20}$$

After inserting the definitions for $\mathbf{T}$, $\mathbf{U}$, and $\mathbf{W}$, we obtain Equations (A.12, A.13, A.12). ■

A.4.1 Derivation of the eNAC1

As we have seen in Section 4.4.3.2 for the estimator g_1, the baseline b can only be a constant, the compatible function approximation is obviously given by

$$f_w(\boldsymbol{\xi}^j) = \left(\sum_{\tau=0}^{N} \nabla_\theta \log \pi(\mathbf{u}_\tau^j|\mathbf{x}_{0:\tau}^j)\right)^T \mathbf{w}, \tag{A.21}$$

for history $\boldsymbol{\xi}^j$ and the targets are the accumulated rewards along the trajectory $r(\boldsymbol{\xi}^j)$. When we bring this into the standard regression form, the basis functions are given by

$$\mathbf{X}^T = \begin{bmatrix} \phi_{1:n}^1, & \phi_{1:n}^2, & \ldots, & \phi_{1:n}^m \\ 1, & 1, & \ldots, & 1 \end{bmatrix}, \tag{A.22}$$

where $\phi_{1:n}^j = \sum_{\tau=0}^{N} \nabla_\theta \log \pi(\mathbf{u}_\tau^j|\mathbf{x}_{0:\tau}^j)$ denotes the log-probability of the j-th roll-out, and the targets are given by

$$\mathbf{Y}^T = \left[r_{1:n}^1, \; r_{1:n}^2, \; \ldots, \; r_{1:n}^m\right], \tag{A.23}$$

where $r_{1:n}^j = r(\boldsymbol{\xi}^j)$ denotes the sum of the rewards of the j-the roll-out. The solution $\beta^* = [\mathbf{w}^T, b]^T$ can then be derived as shown in Theorem A.2.

Theorem A.2 *The solution $\beta^* = [\mathbf{w}_1^T, b_1]^T$ to the regression problem can be given by*

$$\mathbf{w}_1 = \mathbf{F}_1^{-1}\mathbf{g}_1, \tag{A.24}$$

$$b_1 = m^{-1}\left(1 + \bar{\phi}^T\left(m\mathbf{F}_1 - \bar{\phi}\bar{\phi}^T\right)^{-1}\bar{\phi}\right)\left(\bar{r} - \bar{\phi}^T\mathbf{F}_1^{-1}\mathbf{g}\right) \tag{A.25}$$

with Fisher information $\mathbf{F}_1$, average eligibility $\bar{\phi}$, average reward $\bar{r}$,policy gradient with baseline $\mathbf{g}_1$ and without baseline $\mathbf{g}$ given by

$$\mathbf{F}_1 = \sum_{j=1}^{m} \phi_{1:n}^j (\phi_{1:n}^j)^T, \; \bar{\phi} = \sum_{j=1}^{m} \phi_{1:n}^j, \; \bar{r} = \sum_{j=1}^{m} r_{1:n}^j, \tag{A.26}$$

$$\mathbf{g}_1 = \sum_{j=1}^{m} \phi_{1:n}^j \left(r_{1:n}^j - b_1\right), \; \mathbf{g} = \sum_{j=1}^{m} \phi_{1:n}^j r_{1:n}^j. \tag{A.27}$$

Proof. We make use of Theorem A.1 in the Appendix. We first obtain

$$\mathbf{X}_1^T\mathbf{X}_1 = \mathbf{F}_1, \mathbf{X}_1^T\mathbf{X}_2 = \bar{\phi}, \mathbf{X}_2^T\mathbf{X}_2 = m, \mathbf{X}_1^T\mathbf{Y} = \mathbf{g} = \mathbf{g}_1 + \bar{\phi}b, \mathbf{X}_2^T\mathbf{Y} = \bar{r}. \quad \text{(A.28)}$$

We insert these into Equations (A.12, A.13, A.14) from Theorem A.1, and obtain

$$\mathbf{w} = \beta_1 = \mathbf{F}_1^{-1}\left(\mathbf{g} - \bar{\phi}\mathbf{b}\right) = \mathbf{F}_1^{-1}\mathbf{g}_1, \quad \text{(A.29)}$$

$$b = \beta_2 = \mathbf{Q}^{-1}\left(\bar{r} - \bar{\phi}^T\mathbf{F}_1^{-1}\mathbf{g}\right), \quad \text{(A.30)}$$

with $\mathbf{Q}^{-1} = m^{-1}(1 + \bar{\phi}^T(m\mathbf{F}_1 - \bar{\phi}\bar{\phi}^T)^{-1}\bar{\phi})$. ■

Note that this gradient estimator is in fact using exactly the REINFORCE gradient and just one, constant baseline. This can alternatively be derived using Suttons form by adding up the advantages along a path and is also known as episodic natural actor-critic (Peters et al., 2003a; Peters, Vijayakumar, & Schaal, 2003b). As this point, it might appear that we have thrown the child out together with the water as we need the reward sequence to approximate the gradient and at the same time need the gradient to approximate the reward sequence.

A.4.2 Derivation of the eNACn

As we have seen in Section 4.4.3.3 for the estimator $\mathbf{g}_2$, the baseline b depends only on time (and the initial state), the compatible function approximation is obviously given by

$$f_w(\xi_{0:k}^j) = \left(\sum_{\tau=0}^{k} \nabla_\theta \log \pi(u_\tau^j | x_\tau^j)\right)^T w, \quad \text{(A.31)}$$

and the targets are the actual rewards along the trajectory, i.e., $r(\xi_{0:t}) = r_t$. When we bring this into the standard regression form, the basis functions are given by

$$\mathbf{X} = \begin{bmatrix} \phi_{1:1}^1, & \phi_{1:2}^1, & \ldots, & \phi_{1:n}^1, & \phi_{1:1}^2, & \ldots, & \phi_{1:n}^m \\ \mathbf{u}_1, & \mathbf{u}_2, & \ldots, & \mathbf{u}_n, & \mathbf{u}_1, & \ldots, & \mathbf{u}_n \end{bmatrix}, \quad \text{(A.32)}$$

where $\phi_{1:n}^j = \sum_{t=1}^n \nabla_\theta \log \pi(u_t^j | x_t^j)$ denotes the log-probability of the j-th roll-out, and $\mathbf{u}_i$ denotes the i-th unit vector basis function of length n. The targets are given by

$$\mathbf{Y} = \left[r_1^1, \; r_2^1, \; \ldots, \; r_n^1, \; r_1^2, \; \ldots, \; r_n^m\right], \quad \text{(A.33)}$$

where r_t^j denotes the rewards at time t of the j-the roll-out. The solution $\beta^* = [\mathbf{w}^T, b]^T$ can then be derived as shown in Theorem A.3.

Theorem A.3 *The solution $\beta_2^* = [\mathbf{w}_2^T, b_2]^T$ to the regression problem can be given by*

$$\mathbf{w}_2 = \mathbf{F}_2^{-1}\mathbf{g}_2, \quad \text{(A.34)}$$

$$\mathbf{b}_2 = m^{-1}\left(\mathbf{I}_n + \bar{\mathbf{\Phi}}^T\left(m\mathbf{F}_2 - \bar{\mathbf{\Phi}}\bar{\mathbf{\Phi}}^T\right)^{-1}\bar{\mathbf{\Phi}}\right)\left(\bar{\mathbf{r}} - \bar{\mathbf{\Phi}}^T\mathbf{F}_1^{-1}\mathbf{g}\right) \tag{A.35}$$

with Fisher information $\mathbf{F}_1$*, average eligibility* $\bar{\phi}$*, average reward* $\bar{\mathbf{r}}$*, policy gradient with baseline* $\mathbf{g}_1$ *and without baseline* $\mathbf{g}$ *given by*

$$\mathbf{F}_2 = \sum_{j=1}^{m}\sum_{i=1}^{n}\phi_{1:i}^j\left(\phi_{1:i}^j\right)^T, \bar{\mathbf{\Phi}} = \sum_{j=1}^{m}\sum_{i=1}^{n}\phi_{1:i}^j\mathbf{e}_i^T, \bar{\mathbf{r}} = \sum_{j=1}^{m}\sum_{i=1}^{n}r_i^j\mathbf{e}_i, \tag{A.36}$$

$$\mathbf{g}_2 = \sum_{j=1}^{m}\sum_{i=1}^{n}\phi_{1:i}^j\left(r_i^j - b_i\right), \mathbf{g} = \sum_{j=1}^{m}\sum_{i=1}^{n}\phi_{1:i}^j r_i^j. \tag{A.37}$$

Proof. We make use of Theorem A.1 in the Appendix. We first obtain

$$\mathbf{X}_1^T\mathbf{X}_1 = \mathbf{F}_2, \mathbf{X}_1^T\mathbf{X}_2 = \bar{\mathbf{\Phi}}, \mathbf{X}_2^T\mathbf{X}_2 = m\mathbf{I}_n, \mathbf{X}_1^T\mathbf{Y} = \mathbf{g} = \mathbf{g}_2 + \bar{\mathbf{\Phi}}\mathbf{b}_2, \mathbf{X}_2^T\mathbf{Y} = \bar{\mathbf{r}}. \tag{A.38}$$

We insert these into Equations (A.12, A.13, A.14) from Theorem A.1, and obtain

$$\mathbf{w} = \boldsymbol{\beta}_1 = \mathbf{F}_2^{-1}\left(\mathbf{g} - \bar{\mathbf{\Phi}}\mathbf{b}\right) = \mathbf{F}_2^{-1}\mathbf{g}_2, \tag{A.39}$$

$$\mathbf{b} = \beta_2 = \mathbf{Q}^{-1}\left(\bar{r} - \bar{\mathbf{\Phi}}^T\mathbf{F}_2^{-1}\mathbf{g}\right), \tag{A.40}$$

with $\mathbf{Q}^{-1} = m^{-1}(\mathbf{I}_n + \bar{\mathbf{\Phi}}^T(m\mathbf{F}_2 - \bar{\mathbf{\Phi}}\bar{\mathbf{\Phi}}^T)^{-1}\bar{\mathbf{\Phi}})$. ■

Note that this gradient compatible reward estimator is in fact using the GPOMDP gradient with a time-variant scalar baseline b_k.

A.5 Motor Primitive Equations

The motor primitives from (Ijspeert et al., 2002, 2003) in their most recent reformualtion are given by a canonical system

$$\tau^{-1}\dot{v} = \alpha_v\left(\beta_v\left(g - x\right) - v\right), \tag{A.41}$$

$$\tau^{-1}\dot{x} = v, \tag{A.42}$$

which represents the phase of the motor process. It has a goal g, a time constant τ and some parameters α_v,β_v which are chosen so that the system is stable. Additionally, we have a transformed system

$$\tau^{-1}\dot{z} = \alpha_z\left(\beta_z\left(s - x\right) - v\right) + f\left(x, v, g\right), \tag{A.43}$$

$$\tau^{-1}\dot{y} = z, \tag{A.44}$$

$$\tau^{-1}\dot{s} = \alpha_s\left(g - s\right), \tag{A.45}$$

which has the same time-constant τ as the canonical system, appropriately set parameters α_z,β_z,α_s, and a transformation function $f(x, v, g)$. The transformation function transforms the output of the canonical system so that the transformed system can represent complex nonlinear patterns and is given by

$$f(x, v, g) = \frac{\sum_{i=1}^{N} \psi_i(x)\, \theta_i v}{\sum_{i=1}^{N} \psi_i(x)}, \tag{A.46}$$

where θ_i are adjustable parameters and it has localization weights defined by

$$\psi_i(x) = \exp\left(-h_i \left(\frac{x - x_0}{g - x_0} - c_i\right)^2\right) \tag{A.47}$$

with offset x_0, centers c_i and width h_i.

CPSIA information can be obtained
at www.ICGtesting.com
Printed in the USA
LVHW051742041219
639420LV00005B/526/P

9 783639 021103